THE CATHOLIC UNIVERSITY OF AMERICA
CANON LAW STUDIES
Number 87

THE SENTENCE IN ECCLESIASTICAL PROCEDURE

AN HISTORICAL SYNOPSIS AND COMMENTARY

A DISSERTATION

Submitted to the Faculty of Canon Law of the Catholic University of America in Partial Fulfillment of the Requirements for the Degree of

DOCTOR OF CANON LAW

BY

DELISLE ANTOINE LEMIEUX, M.A., J.C.L.,
Priest of the Diocese of Denver

THE CATHOLIC UNIVERSITY OF AMERICA
WASHINGTON, D. C.
1934.

Nihil Obstat:

VALENTINUS T. SCHAAF, O.F.M., J.C.D.,
Censor Deputatus.

Washingtonii, D. C., die xix Maii, 1934.

Imprimatur:

URBANUS J. VEHR, D.D.,
Episcopus Denveriensis.

Denveri, die xxii Maii, 1934.

Printed by
THE PAULIST PRESS
New York, N. Y.

TO

MY MOTHER

CONTENTS

CHAPTER VII

CHAPTER VIII

FOREWORD

THE sentence offers a pertinent and an appropriate subject for a treatise in Canon Law, not so much because of difficult questions, but rather on account of its practical importance in ecclesiastical procedure. The object of all law is to establish justice in human relations, and the sentence is the real application *in fact* of justice to the individual members of society by judiciary power. It might be loosely defined as that which is officially judged as *just* in a particular case. "Causa a casu, quo venit, dicitur. Est enim materia et origo negotii, necdum discussionis examine patefacta; quae, dum proponitur, causa est; dum discutitur, iudicium; dum finitur, iustitia . . . iudex dictus quasi ius dicens populo." [1] Thus a notable part is taken by the sentence in the process, and it assumes proportions of real importance. It becomes the focal point to which the whole process of applying law is directed, and if it is not properly constituted, the whole process is in vain and the purpose of law is frustrated. From the standpoint of jurisprudence, the sentence in early Roman and Canon law procedure has contributed much to the knowledge, development, and practical application of law. The study of the ecclesiastical legislation on the sentence often affords an advantageous vista from which to gain a more profound understanding of the Church's sound philosophy of law.

The purpose of this dissertation is to treat of the sentence in canonical procedure as regards its nature, object, form, content, publication, and effect according to Canons 1868 to 1877 of the Code. The treatment of these subjects will be handled with the view of giving some helpful and practical appreciation of the sentence in its composition and function. Excepting perhaps the treatment of some of its internal qualities as moral certitude and motivation, the sentence offers little difficulty to clear interpretation according to the Code. Many practical points are to be found in questions pertaining

[1] C. 10, X, *De Verborum significatione*, V. 40.

to prescription against the sentence, nullity of the sentence, the sentence in collegiate tribunals, and the various kinds of trials.

The dissertation has been divided into two parts. The purpose of the first part will be to clarify some of the preliminary notions, to indicate some of the stages of development, and to give an historical background to the present legislation. One of the chief sources to be considered will be Roman law, since it is from this form of the sentence that many prescriptions of Canon Law are modeled. There is a great amount of pertinent matter to be found in the past legislation of the Church. Much of this will be helpful for later commentary. From the past legislation it is desired to quote important points which have had a bearing upon the development of the present legislation. Not a great deal has been added to the fundamental notion of the sentence as found in Roman law, but much has been added in the way of perfecting the concise application of law and of preserving justice. Of necessity this part will be brief in attempting to give a general outline on the points stated above, and by no means will it pretend to give an exhaustive treatment of the history, but simply a short historical conspectus.

The second part is devoted to a commentary on the general prescriptions of the Code on the sentence. Herein, it is intended to give a juridic survey of the present legislation with the aim of affording some practical assistance to those actively interested in ecclesiastical judicial procedure. It is presumed that the reader has some knowledge of Canon Law. Hence an exhaustive didactic treatment, especially on common principles of procedure, is not considered necessary. In the interpretation of the present law, an effort has been made to seek sound opinions and indices to the solution of controverted points from the more recent of the recognized commentators on procedure.

This occasion is taken to express profound gratitude to the Most Reverend Urban J. Vehr, D.D., Bishop of Denver, for the opportunity of advanced study which His Excellency in promoting clerical scholarship has afforded to the writer. The writer wishes also to acknowledge sincere appreciation to the members of the Faculty of the School of Canon Law for their generous assistance in preparation of this work and to express his appreciation of the many courtesies extended to him by librarians of the University Library.

CHAPTER I

PRELIMINARY NOTIONS

ART. 1. ORIGIN AND USE OF TERM

BEFORE taking up the definitions on the subject, it is necessary to consider a few preliminary notions about the sentence. The term was used in early Roman law. In the earliest beginnings it was the declaration of a private person acting as arbiter in settling disputes. His decision was called "sententia," *i. e.*, an opinion. This seems to have been the origin of the application of the term to judicial procedure, because later the legal significance developed when this form of arbitration was given legal force in Roman Law development. The sentence then became a true judgment, a judicial pronouncement applying the law with legal force.[1] Thus in treating of Roman law, Sohm [2] frequently uses the terms, judgment and sentence, as interchangeable. In Canon law the term *sentence* is used to designate the final pronouncement of the judge in every case, criminal or contentious, of judicial process. The same usage is not followed in our secular courts in which it is applied to only one of three forms of judicial process. The practice of the secular courts in designating the final judicial pronouncement is as follows: for the criminal courts, *a sentence;* for the court of equity, *a decree;* and for the court of law, *a judgment.* In the manner of procedure, the court of equity affords the nearest approach to the judicial procedure of Canon law.

It is of interest to note a fundamental distinction in the nature of the sentence based on a variance of the two great systems of procedure, Germanic and Roman, as they first began to be formulated. In the Roman notion the sentence was a declaration of right—(nonnisi inter partes *ius* dicebat); whereas the Germanic law followed the notion of popular deliberation—(conventu populi emissa).[3] Canon

[1] Engelmann, *A History of Continental Civil Procedure,* sec. 80, p. 362.

[2] *The Institutes of Roman Law.*

[3] Roberti, *De Processibus,* n. 1.

law adopted the Roman concept of the sentence. The inherent weaknesses of "popular deliberation" with its vacillations, emotional excitability, and morbid sentimentality are only too evident today in the jury system of our civil courts. Perhaps it is the best method for the civil administration of justice in practice but from a juridic standpoint the method of ecclesiastical procedure is superior. What will function properly in one sphere might not do so in the other because the Church stands on a higher moral plane than civil government, and she can establish the proper constitution and exercise authority where others fail.

There are two elements in the sentence which should be considered: *the reasoning* and *the legal command* of the judge; one on the part of his *understanding*, and the other on the part of his *will*. Through the judicial process the judge seeks to establish the truth, and then he applies it as a legal command. Both elements are to be found in every law, but *formally* the law consists in the command or order of constituted authority—(ratio legis non est lex). By applying the law in a concrete case in the sentence, the judge declares his *will* on the law. Hence the sentence may be rightly called a "special law." If the other element (objective justice) is entirely lacking, the sentence is to be considered invalid. In Roman law the chief consideration was the revealing of the *will* of the judge, and secondly his *reasonings*. In Canon law one or the other of these two elements prevails in the sentence according as the cause may or may not become *res iudicata* (irrevocably adjudged). Thus in causes concerning the state of persons (*status personarum*), as matrimony, holy orders, and religious profession, which never become *res iudicata,*[4] the prime element is to establish *the truth* because in spiritual matters the objective truth must prevail.[5]

The sentence is the principal means of concluding the process. Ordinarily, after the close of the trial, *i. e.*, after the hearing of proofs and the final defense of the cause, it necessarily follows that the cause

[4] Noval, *De Processibus,* n. 675; Dec. XIX, n. 4, *Sanctae Romanae Rotae Decisiones seu Sententiae* (1922).

[5] *Cf.* Roberti, *De Processibus,* n. 443; Coronata, *De Processibus,* n. 1393.

be settled by the sentence. *Ordinarily* because there are other ways by which the process may be concluded, namely: by agreement (Canons 1925 ff.), by arbitration (Canons 1929 ff.), by abatement (Canons 1736 ff.), by withdrawal of complaint (Canons 1740 ff.), by the case being discharged (Canon 1850, § 3).[6] Excepting these cases, the judicial process is to be concluded by the pronouncing of sentence. It is to be noted that in causes in which proof is established by decisive oath (Canons 1834 ff.), by judicial confession (Canons 1750 ff.), or by notorious facts (Canon 1747), sentence is to be pronounced.[7]

In concluding the process, the sentence serves to apply the law of the Church in a particular concrete instance.[8] It becomes the conclusion of the legal syllogism. Thus the particular application of the law is deduced as follows: The provisions of ecclesiastical legislation is the major; the declaration and proof of facts according to judicial rules, the minor; and the sentence is the conclusion. This simple comparison gives a clear idea of the purpose of the sentence. Once the cause is properly tried the judge cannot refrain from passing sentence.[9]

The first recorded prescription on the sentence is to be found in the Code of Hammurabi, which was drawn up in about 2250 B. C.

> If a judge pronounce a judgment, render a decision, deliver a verdict duly signed and sealed and afterward alter his judgment, they shall call that judge to account for the alteration of the judgment which he had pronounced, and he shall pay twelvefold the penalty which was in said judgment; and, in the assembly, they shall expel him from his seat of judgment, and he shall not return, and with the judges in a case he shall not take his seat.[10]

This provision made the sentence, once it was properly imposed,

[6] Noval, *De Processibus,* n. 618; Roberti, *De Processibus,* n. 442.

[7] Roberti, *De Processibus,* n. 442.

[8] C. 10, X, *de verborum significatione,* V. 40.

[9] Muniz, *Procedimientos Eclesiasticos,* n. 439; Wernz-Vidal, *De Processibus,* n. 589.

[10] *Code of Hammurabi,* § 5.

irrevocable. By implication it is evident that it was to be drawn up in written form, signed by the judge and stamped with the proper seal.

This prescription is mentioned merely for its historical interest. It has no bearing on the development of ecclesiastical legislation.

Art. 2. Divisions and Definitions (Canon 1868)

> **Canon 1868, § 1. Legitima pronuntiatio qua iudex causam a litigantibus propositam et iudiciali modo pertractatam definit, sententia est: eaque *interlocutoria* dicitur, si dirimat incidentem causam; *definitiva*, si principalem.**
>
> **§ 2. Ceterae iudicis pronuntiationes *decreta* vocantur.**

Canon 1868 classifies the acts of judgment as definitive and interlocutory sentences and decrees. The same classification is observed in the Rota,[11] although four acts are enumerated, viz., definitive and interlocutory sentences, decrees and rescripts. The reason is that under the term *decree* the Code includes what is termed *rescripts* in the *Regulae* of the Rota.[12] From the Code then there are two kinds of judicial pronouncements, sentences and decrees.

The word "sentence" is derived from "*sentire*"—to think. Hence it is the opinion of the judge considering the cause. From the proofs of the cause, he forms his own conscientious conviction,[13] and this he declares in the sentence. The pronouncement of the judge is what he thinks about the cause in question or controversy before him.[14]

The sentence is defined in Canon 1868, § 1, of the Code as a "legitimate pronouncement by which the judge decides a case pro-

[11] *Regulae servandae in iudiciis apud S. R. Rotae Tribunal,* § 79, n. 3—*AAS,* II (1910), 809.

[12] Coronata, *De Processibus,* n. 1395.

[13] C. 6, X, *de renuntiatione,* I, 9.

[14] Reiffenstuel, *Ius Canonicum,* II, 27, n. 6; Lega, *De Iudiciis Ecclesiasticis,* n. 602.

posed by the litigants and tried in judicial form." [15] Enlarging upon this definition, the sentence must be a pronouncement given according to the sacred canons by a judge having the proper jurisdiction, and it must settle the issue of the controversy. The pronouncement must be based on legitimate proofs, be given in legal form, and it must be evolved in judicial manner, *i. e.*, by way of legal dispute of contradictory claims.[16]

"Causa" should be translated "cause." "Cause" specifically signifies a matter of judicial nature.[17] "Causa est res seu ius deductum in iudicium." [18] The term "case," from which "cause" is drawn, is more comprehensive.

Sentences are either *definitive* or *interlocutory*. This general division of sentences into these two kinds is of great practical import and is definitely propounded by Canon 1868. "The sentence is called interlocutory, if it decides an incidental cause; it is called definitive, if it settles the principal cause." [19]

§ 1. *The Definitive Sentence*

The definitive sentence is one which decides the cause or controversy itself; to be more precise, it settles the issue which was primarily and directly instituted by the plaintiff or *actor* and not a question arising during the proceedings.[20] In a general sense the definitive sentence has a twofold division in all causes, namely: *Absolutory*, which is favorable to the defendant or *reus* and unfavorable to the plaintiff or *actor; Condemnatory*, which is unfavorable to the defendant and favorable to the plaintiff.[21] However in criminal causes the condemnatory sentence is subdivided as follows: *Simple Condemnatory*, which convicts the defendant and *now* inflicts the penalty which was not inflicted before although ordained

[15] Translation by Woywod, *A Practical Commentary on the Code of Canon Law*, n. 1791.

[16] Noval, *De Processibus*, n. 620.

[17] C. 10, X, *de verborum significatione*, V. 40.

[18] Vives, *Compendium Juris Canonici*, p. 409.

[19] *Cf.* Roberti, *De Processibus*, n. 444-445; Coronata, *De Processibus*, n. 1394.

[20] Noval, *De Processibus*, n. 620; Reiffenstuel, *op. cit.*, II, t. 27, n. 9.

[21] *Cf.* Canon 1873, § 1, n. 1.

by law; *Declaratory,* which pronounces the crime to have been committed and is retroactive in regard to the penalty, establishing that it was incurred *by the very fact* at the moment that the crime was perpetrated.[22]

The absolutory sentence may be one of two kinds: *absolutoria ab observatione iudicii,* which relieves the defendant from the present instance but not from further action by the *actor; absolutoria ab impetitione actoris,* which definitively frees the defendant from the action of the *actor.*[23]

Question is raised as to whether or not there is in Canon law such a thing as a constitutive sentence (*sententia constitutiva*), that is, one intermediate to a condemnatory and a declaratory sentence. It contains more than a mere declaration of a past fact made in a declaratory sentence, and nevertheless its effects are had without the execution required in a condemnatory sentence. The effects, while they depend upon some provision of law, seem to be established by the force of the sentence itself, and thereby the sentence does more than apply the law in that it seems to establish the rights of the party. Thus for instance, a favorable sentence in a rescissory action [24] is said to establish the rights of the petitioner. This theory seems to have no place in canon law because the judge has no power to constitute rights. Therefore, the juridic effect of a sentence supporting a rescissory action is to be considered as applying a right established by law.[25]

§ 2. *The Interlocutory Sentence*

The *interlocutory* sentence is one, as the term signifies, which the judge pronounces (*loquitur*) between (*inter*) the beginning of the trial and the definitive sentence to settle, not the principal cause,

[22] Coronata, *De Processibus,* n. 1394; *cf.* Schmalzgrueber, *Ius Ecclesiasticum,* II, t. 27, n. 18; Reiffenstuel, *op. cit.,* II, t. 27, n. 12 ff.; Bouix, *Tractatus de Iud. Eccl.,* II, p. 224; Canon 2232, § 2.

[23] Noval, *De Processibus,* n. 619.

[24] Canons 1684 ff.

[25] *Cf.* Roberti, *De Processibus,* n. 447; Coronata, *De Processibus,* n. 1394.

but some incidental cause or point which arises and must be decided before the trial can proceed.[26] It is divided into two classes: the *simple,* and the *mixed* or one having definitive force. The *simple* interlocutory sentence is one that settles some incidental cause or point but has no determining effect on the final decision so as to virtually settle it. The interlocutory sentence with *definitive force* while only deciding an incidental cause, is such that it materially affects the main issue and in such a way as to virtually decide it. Though it does not actually settle the main issue, still it indirectly determines its solution.[27] This is called a prejudicial sentence.

§ 3. *Decrees*

"Other pronouncements of the judge are called decrees." [28]

A decree might be defined in a negative sense as any pronouncement of the judge which is not a sentence.[29] In a positive sense, commands, orders, and prohibitions, which are not based on a legal dispute of the litigants and do not judicially close the cause, are classified as *decrees.*[30] The fundamental difference between decrees and sentences seems to be in this: that in issuing a decree the judge does not observe the requirements of judicial trial.[31] Canonists writing before the Code classified as interlocutory sentences, many pronouncements which are now recognized by the Code as decrees.[32] Decrees given in judicial procedure are *judicial decrees;* those given in administrative procedure are *administrative decrees.*

Roberti distinguishes two kinds of judicial decrees: *ordinatoria,* and *decisoria.* The ordinating decrees (*ordinatoria*) are those which

[26] Wernz-Vidal, *De Processibus,* n. 587.

[27] Smith, *Ecclesiastical Trials,* n. 1155; Vermeersch-Creusen, *Epitome Juris Canonici,* III, n. 228.

[28] Canon 1868, § 2.

[29] Roberti, *De Processibus,* I, n. 188.

[30] "Hae pronuntiationes [decreta] sunt iussa, ordinationes, prohibitiones, quae in contradictorio litigantium non nituntur nec causam iudicialiter dirimunt." Vermeersch-Creusen, *op. cit.,* III, n. 228.

[31] Blat, *De Processibus,* n. 361.

[32] Coronata, *De Processibus,* n. 1395; *cf.* Smith, *Ecclesiastical Trials,* n. 1156.

govern the process. They do not touch on the merit of the question, regularly suppose no contestation, and contain only the disposition, *i. e.*, the judicial command. The decisive decrees (*decisoria*) settle some incidental question. They contain besides the disposition, reasons in fact and in law, and they suppose some sort of contestation. It is left to the discretion of the judge whether to settle incidental cases by an interlocutory sentence or by a decree.[33]

No appeal is admitted from a decree of the judge except in those cases expressly stated by law.[34] For example, a judge's decree in favor of his competence admits of no appeal; but a decree against his competence may be appealed within ten days.[35]

It might be well to note here that the final pronouncement of the judge settling a case where the rules of judicial procedure are observed is a sentence. The legal requirements of the sentence are to be observed in criminal trials, Matrimonial trials, the Documentary process,[36] causes against Sacred Ordination, the Canonization process,[37] and the process for the dismissal of exempt religious,[38] whereas, the special modes of administrative procedure as contained in the Third Part of Book IV of the Code, are settled by a decree.[39]

[33] Canon 1840, § 1; Roberti, *De Processibus,* I, n. 188.

[34] *Cf.* Canon 1880, n. 6.

[35] Canon 1610, §§ 2, 3.

[36] Kay, *Competence in Matrimonial Procedure,* p. 152.

[37] *Cf.* Noval, *De Processibus,* II, n. 1-5.

[38] *Cf.* Schaefer, *De Religiosis,* n. 593.

[39] *Cf.* Noval, *De Processibus,* III, nn. 442, 462; Augustine enumerates a list of the decrees as determined by the Code. Augustine, *A Commentary on the New Code of Canon Law,* vol. VII, appendix II.

CHAPTER II

THE SENTENCE IN ROMAN LAW

Art. 1. Relation Between Canon Law and Roman Law

Because much of the legal prescription on the sentence is drawn from Roman law, it will be important to give a brief survey of the relation of Canon and Roman law procedure.

With the Church from the first moments of her existence exercising her legislative power, it became necessary in the enforcement of her laws that some form of judicial procedure be employed. At first this was, no doubt, a very simple form dictated by circumstances of incipient development. The cases of Ananias and Saphira might be cited as an example of it. In the case of Ananias there is scarcely evident any judicial form, but in the case of Saphira it is distinguishable in vague outline. She is brought before the judge, accused, confesses her guilt by silence, and is sentenced.[1] Other instances in Sacred Scripture indicate some form of judicial procedure; viz., 1 Timothy, V, 19; 1 Cor., VI, 1. The bishops, succeeding the Apostles, filled the role of judge for the faithful; more as arbiters in small controversies, but as real judges in spiritual affairs. With the ending of the early persecutions and the attaining of official recognition by the Church from the civil power, the phenomenal growth of the Church brought a great increase in cases brought before the Ecclesiastical forum. This necessitated a gradual extension and better systematization of ecclesiastical procedure. In effecting this development, the Church chose much from Roman law which thus became a subsidiary source of Canon law. "For the codification of its laws the Church is deeply indebted to the ancient civil systems, especially of Rome." [2]

[1] *Acts,* V, 1 ff.

[2] Van Hove, *Prolegomena,* n. 91; *cf.* Devoti, *Institutionum Canonicarum,* lib. IV, t. I ff.; *Catholic Encyclopedia,* "Ecclesiastical Courts."

While the Church borrowed much of its judicial procedure from the ancient civil system, it is pertinent to note that the Church's judicial power was always inherent in the Church itself. The Church was established for the purpose of achieving the sanctification and eternal salvation of mankind. It originated by the will of God, and it has as its actual founder God in the person of Jesus Christ. By Him it was endowed with the necessary means to attain its end and thereby established as a perfect society with inherent power to teach, to govern and to sanctify. Its governing power is, therefore, of divine right. The Church being a perfect society enjoys the threefold governing power, legislative, judicial, and executive, over its adherents. This power is supreme in its own sphere and is independent of any civil power. The Church therefore has real judicial power from the institution of its Divine Founder.[3] Historically, there is abundant evidence of the Church's consciousness of this power and the continual exercise thereof from her earliest beginnings, as narrated in the New Testament, down to the present time.

The Church acted prudently in borrowing from the ancient legal systems. As she did not hesitate to appropriate the best of pagan cultural attainments in the art and philosophy of Greece and Rome and then proceed to inject into them a new vitality and nobler purpose and to develop them to greater heights of perfection, so she likewise appropriated the legal cultural attainments of Rome, and adding a new impulse raised them to a state of greater excellence.[4] Had the exigency existed, no doubt the Church would have developed a legal system distinctively her own. But characteristically she incorporated that which was at hand and modified it to serve her purposes. This was consummate wisdom because Rome's greatest contribution to civilization was her law. There is found a survival of Roman law in all civilized nations of the world today.[5] Roman law, with its centralization of power, was peculiarly adapted to the gov-

[3] Cappello, *Summa Iuris Publici Ecclesiastici*, n. 180; Van Hove, *De Legibus*, n. 83 ff.; Chelodi, *Jus de Personis*, n. 19; Devoti, *Institutionum Canonicarum*, lib. IV, t. I ff.; *Catholic Encyclopedia*, "Ecclesiastical Courts."

[4] Roberti, *De Processibus*, n. 2; Maroto, *Institutiones Iuris Canonici*, I, n. 380.

[5] Sherman, *Roman Law in the Modern World*, I, sec. 11.

ernment of the Church because of the authority invested by Christ in the supreme head of the Church, the Pope. It was also recommended by its natural equity. Then, too, a logical implication would be that because of the fact that the Theodosian Code and later the Justinian Code and Novels conferred certain judicial power upon the bishops in the secular forum, there was brought about a natural rapprochement of the church and civil procedure which tended to cause an assimilation of many points of the civil procedure into the ecclesiastical.

Since the Church has been depicted as a borrower of legal culture, it is fitting that her contributions to legal culture be indicated at least in a general way. While Roman law attained great heights of natural perfection,[6] still as with all human law it left much to be desired. A few quotations from many possible ones will serve to throw light on the high natural philosophy underlying Roman law.

> There is a true law conformable to justice, diffused through all hearts, unchangeable, eternal, which by its commands summons to duty, by its prohibitions deters from evil.[7]
>
> Nomen iuris est autem a iustitia appellatum . . . ius est ars boni et aequi.[8]
>
> Justice is the constant and enduring will to render to everyone his just dues . . . the precepts of the law are these, to live uprightly, not to injure a neighbor, and to render to everyone his own.[9]

In practice human society needs more than the light of reason. The Church has this "something more" in the revelation and the teachings of her Founder, the Author of Justice, Jesus Christ. With these divine influences in the background it was to be expected that the Church would contribute much to the elevation of the legal culture of the world.

> The work of Christianity was to perfect the system of law erected upon such a solid foundation, by adding to the beauty of the super-structure, strengthening it by removing

[6] Sherman, *op. cit.*, I, sec. 3; II, sec. 420 ff.

[7] Cicero, *De Republica*, III, 22.

[8] *D.* 1, 1, 1.

[9] *D.* 1, 1, 10.

structural weaknesses, and enlarging or transforming Roman Law in the spirit of Christian ethics so as to produce greater justice and benefit to mankind.[10]

The influence of Christianity was very efficient toward the introduction of a better and more enlightened sense of right and justice among the governments of Europe. It taught the duty of benevolence to strangers, of humanity to the vanquished, of the obligation of good faith, and of the sin of murder, revenge, and rapacity. The Church had its councils or convocations of the clergy, which formed the nations professing Christianity into a connection resembling a federal alliance; and those councils sometimes settled the titles and claims of princes, and regulated the temporal affairs of the Christian powers. The confederacy of the Christian nations was bound together by a sense of common duty and interest, in respect to the rest of mankind.[11]

Art. 2. The Sentence in Roman Civil Procedure

Since Canon Law adopted the general form of its procedure from Roman Law procedure, it is necessary in giving the historical background of practically all phases of Canon law procedure to trace the origin and development of these phases in Roman law. This is particularly true of the sentence because of its similarity in both procedures. In a cursory manner, therefore, a few salient points will be touched on the legal requirements of the sentence and on its nature and form in Roman law. Many of the directive principles are helpful for the understanding and interpretation of the Canon law.

Roman civil procedure readily divides itself into three distinct periods. The *first period* dates from the beginning of Rome until about 150 B. C., and the system of procedure used herein was known as the "statute actions" (*legis actiones*) of the early Republic (from the time of XII Tables until about 150 B. C.) The *second period* includes from 150 B. C. until about 300 A. D. (later Republic and early Empire). The procedure of this period was known as the *formulary* or *ordinary* procedure. The *third period* (later Empire) dates from

[10] Sherman, *op. cit.*, I, sec. 147.

[11] Devereux, *Kent's Commentaries*, p. 5.

about 300 A. D. until post-Justinian times (565 A. D.). This period followed what was known as the *extraordinary* procedure.[12]

In the XII Tables there were incorporated certain "statute actions" (*legis actiones*), *i. e.*, the actions by which cases were to be admitted to trial. The sentence was pronounced by an officially appointed judge. Historical details of the method are meagre. The magistrate was petitioned for the appointment of a judge according to one of the "statute actions." After the appointment the judge filled the role of an arbiter. This was a vestige of the original method of private arbitration. The issue was given orally and was based on the action. After hearing the case and coming to a decision in the matter, the judge pronounced the sentence which simply states whether or not the penalty is properly to be applied.[13]

In the formulary procedure which began to come into existence about 150 B. C., is found one fundamentally similar to the "statute actions." The principal difference between the two was in the procedure of placing the claim in court. In the formulary procedure the magistrate was petitioned for a formula by which the matter was to be adjudicated. The magistrate then gave the formula with certain directions to the judge, who pronounced the sentence after the hearing.[14]

In these periods there are two sharply distinguished phrases of procedure; the session *in jure* and the session *in iudicio*. The session *in jure* was held to give the formulation of the legal issue. Here no sentence is pronounced but only an order of the magistrate granting the submission of the case for a decision *in iudicio* before a judge. Then in the session *in iudicio*, where the case is contested, the decision of the judge in settling it is a true sentence.[15] The sentence is based on the facts and evidence of the case and the conscientious conviction of the judge. The effect of the sentence was twofold: while it had no executive force in itself, it could be brought before the magistrate by *actio iudicati* for the compulsory enforcement; secondly, the sentence established the case "irrevocably adjudged" (*res*

[12] Collinet et Gifford, *Précis de Droit Romain*, I, n. 112.

[13] Collinet et Gifford, *op. cit.*, I, sec. 145; Engelmann, *op. cit.*, sec. 80.

[14] Sohm, *op. cit.*, p. 256.

[15] Sohm, *op. cit.*, p. 225 ff.

iudicata). "Res iudicata dicitur, quae finem controversiarum pronuntiatione iudicis accipit."[16] With the pronouncement of the sentence the case was settled once and for all, and could not be revised or reopened.[17]

The legal procedure of the Later Empire was known as the extraordinary procedure. Only the official of the Emperor could occupy the office of Judge, and the offices of magistrate and judge became one. The arbitral nature of the sentence was lost; which change, as a matter of fact, started in some cases at the beginning of the Empire. The distinction between the session *in iure* and the session *in iudicio* no longer exists, as the latter was absorbed into the former. The decisions now became real sentences which decided the controversy and had executive force. Also a system of appeals from the sentence of a lower official to a higher official was developed. Legal regulations of this period on the sentence will be treated later under the prescriptions of Justinian law.

Art. 3. The Sentence in Roman Criminal Procedure

The Collegiate tribunal played an important part in Roman criminal procedure, particularly during the Republic. Criminal jurisdiction was generally exercised by a group of judges. The cases reserved to them were known as the *quaestiones perpetuae*, and brought under their authority nearly all crimes. The judges were very much like our present jurors. They were chosen from a qualified group of private citizens, and received appointment for each case. Presiding was either a magistrate or pro-magistrate (*quaesitor*). It was the function of the jury after the evidence had been concluded, to give the decision by ballot. To reach a verdict a simple majority vote of the jury was necessary. Originally the jury could render any one of three verdicts: "guilty" (*condemno*), "not guilty" (*absolvo*), or "doubtful" (*non liquet*). Later only one of the first two verdicts (guilty or not guilty) was to be given. If the penalty was variable according to law, the jury could determine the specific penalty in the sentence. A tie vote in cases involving freedom operated in favor

[16] *D.* 42, 1, 1.

[17] *Cf.* Sohm, *op. cit.*, sec. 49, 50; Collinet et Gifford, *op. cit.*, n. 204; Costa, *Profilo Storico del Processo Civile Romano*, p. 79; Engelmann, *op. cit.*, sec. 82.

of the person asserting freedom; and in all other cases it was construed in favor of the defendant. The *quaesitor* pronounced it formally as the decision of the court.[18]

During the third century of the Empire the collegiate tribunal disappeared, after being superseded by the tribunal of one judge, who was the official representative of the Emperor. This marks the beginning of the third period of Roman procedure. Since this tribunal had jurisdiction in both criminal and civil cases, the legal prescription of this period on the sentence applies to both criminal and civil procedure.

Art. 4. Legal Regulations on the Sentence in Justinian Law

Justinian law recognizes two kinds of sentences: *condemnatory,* which settles the issue in favor of the plaintiff (*actor*) and against the defendant (*reus*); *absolutory,* which absolves the defendant. "A definitive sentence which does not contain absolution or condemnation is to be considered null." [19] Savigny [20] mentions a "mixed sentence," which is a combination of the two. He refers to a controversy about what appears to be a third kind of sentence which occurs in two cases, in "duplex actio" and "reconventio." "It appears that there is a third kind of sentence, namely, condemnation of the plaintiff (*actor*); but in these cases the condemnation is not placed against the plaintiff as plaintiff but as defendant (*reus*). Since there are really but two sentences, the principle of not condemning the plaintiff stands, as does also the twofold division."

While Roman law admitted but one judgment, the way for it might be prepared by preliminary and interlocutory orders. They pertained either to the conduct of the cause or to the settlement of incidental questions. Constantine prohibited appeals from these interlocutory orders.[21] Further prohibitions are found in provisions of law in the Theodosian Code [22] and in Justinian law.[23]

[18] Sherman, *op. cit.*, II, sec. 934 ff.; *ibid.*, sec. 880; Engelmann, *op. cit.*, sec. 81, p. 364.

[19] *Cod.* 7, 45, 3.

[20] Savigny, *Sistema del Diritto Romano Attuale,* VI, p. 286.

[21] Engelmann, *op. cit.*, Roman Procedure, sec. 81-85.

[22] *Theodosian Code,* 11, 36, 18.

[23] *Cod.* 7, 62, 36.

Numerous safeguards to preserve the internal quality of justice in the sentence are constituted by precepts of law. "It is of prime importance to note first that a judge may not judge otherwise than it is appointed in the laws or constitutions or customs." [24] " . . . If a sentence is evidently against the force of the law it is invalid." [25]

The sentence was pronounced orally in the presence of the parties. "In every case the sentence ought to be pronounced with all present who are interested in it; . . . If the parties, being informed, were unwilling to appear, a sentence could be passed." [26] If the parties were contumaciously absent, the sentence pronounced could attain status of *res iudicata;* it did not otherwise. Three peremptory orders were to be given for appearance.[27] The sentence was set down in writing.[28] The sentence was void if given on holidays.[29]

Motivation of the sentence was not demanded, and the sentence was given without the sustaining reasons. "In the sentence it suffices to declare the sum to be paid or that what is sought is to be rendered." [30] The sentence pronounced should be clear and definite in regard to the penalty or what was to be done or not done; otherwise it would be of little avail.[31] It should be possible of execution. "An impossible precept of the judge is null." [32] A sentence based on a conditional clause was not recognized as valid.[33]

On the question of expenses, the law ordained that the loser was to pay the winner of the case for the costs entailed. "[Omnes iudices] scient in expensarum causa victum victori esse condemnandum quantum pro solutis expensis litium iuraverit." [34]

[24] *Inst.* 4, 17.
[25] *D.* 49, 1, 19.
[26] *D.* 42, 1, 47.
[27] *Cod.* 7, 43, 1 ff.; *cf.* Costa, *op. cit.*, p. 76, sec. 8.
[28] *Cod.* 7, 44, 3.
[29] *Cod.* 7, 43, 4; *Cod.* 3, 12, 9.
[30] *D.* 42, 1, 59; *cf.* Costa, *op. cit.*, p. 76, sec. 8.
[31] *Inst.* 4, 6 (32).
[32] *D.* 49, 8, 3.
[33] *D.* 49, 4, 1 (5).
[34] *Cod.* 3, 1, 13.

CHAPTER III

CONSPECTUS OF ECCLESIASTICAL LEGISLATION BEFORE THE CODE

Art. 1. The Sentence in the Early Church

While considerable legislation on ecclesiastical procedure is to be found in the history of the early Church, but little detailed regulation of the sentence is available. The exercise of judicial power by the bishops was at first in quite simple form of procedure, which gradually evolved and developed itself. It was only natural to expect that minute legal prescription on the various parts of procedure like the sentence would only come in the due course of time. The chief consideration in regard to judicial procedure that occupied the attention of the early Bishops with their manifold labors, was to administer strict justice for the body of the faithful. There are numerous instances in which the bishops declare the sentence of excommunication in trials of heretics. Let it suffice here to note one or two points about the sentence and the adoption from Roman law of regulations in its regard.

The sentence given by St. Peter in the case of Saphira was pronounced no doubt most solemnly, but with strikingly simple formality. "Behold the feet of them who have buried thy husband are at the door, and they shall carry thee out." [1] It was to be expected that the Apostles in their judicial acts would observe a very simple form of process.

With the growth of the Church, and particularly after the time of Constantine, there was a concomitant growth in the legal regulation of procedure in the canonical trials. The Church in the early centuries found many trying issues to meet in her external forum. The human element often proved to be only too human. The records of the more serious controversies have been handed down to us. From these will be quoted a few instances to indicate the exercise of judicial process and its development. Before the dawn of the second

[1] *Acts* V, 9.

century Pope Clement was called upon to settle dissension at Corinth. In a formal sentence he reprimanded the Corinthians and restored to office the *presbyteri* whom they had ejected.[2] In the second century the impious Marcion was expelled from the clergy.[3] Tertullian bears witness to the use of judicial power and the pronouncement of sentence by the ecclesiastical authorities.[4] St. Cyprian gives similar testimony.[5] Sentence in true judicial form was pronounced against Arius at the Council of Nice (325) and against Nestorius in the Council of Ephesus (431). Many other instances might be cited in which the sentence of excommunication was imposed by the bishops.

Provisions to assure that the sentence of excommunication was just were made at the Council of Nice (326).[6] In Canon 15 of the Council of Antioch (341) the bishops legislated that, if a bishop was accused of some crime and was condemned by the bishops of the province with all concurring in the same sentence, he was to be tried no further by others; the sentence of the bishops of the province definitely settled the case.[7] The sentence of excommunication against a priest or deacon imposed by their proper bishop was operative even when recourse was had against it to the metropolitan see where it could be confirmed or corrected.[8] The bishops were to inflict the sentence of excommunication against those of the laity striving for the higher life who persisted in not properly observing vows of chastity. For clerics the penalty included privation of office. These regulations were ordained by Canon 3 of the Council of Carthage (348),[9] and it indicates that even the laity were often tried for various abuses against Christian life by their bishops. An unjust sentence was void, and it was to be reversed. Sentence was not to be passed in the absence of the accused. These two provisions are declared in Canons 28 and 30 respectively of the Fourth Council of Carthage (398).[10]

[2] *MPG,* I, 199.
[3] *MPG,* XLI, 695.
[4] *MPL,* I, 467.
[5] *MPL,* III, 795.
[6] C. 5—Mansi, *Sacrorum Conciliorum Nova et Amplissima Collectio,* II, 679.
[7] Mansi, II, 1314.
[8] Council of Sardica (344), C. 17—Mansi, III, 28.
[9] Mansi, III, 146.
[10] Mansi, III, 953.

That judicial proof was necessary before sentence could be imposed, is evident from regulations provided in the Seventh Council of Carthage (419). A bishop could not condemn a priest who retracted a private confession unless crime was properly proved.[11] Contentious causes between clerics were tried exclusively by their proper bishops.[12] Justinian law recognized the privilege forum of clerics and religious so that suits against them were to be tried by their bishops in the first instance.[13]

The foregoing provisions, chosen from among many, show clearly that the bishops frequently found it necessary to exercise their judicial power. At their convocations rules of procedure were made in order that uniformity might be established in ecclesiastical trials and justice preserved. It was to be expected that the legislation of this period on the sentence would be concerned with the more basic and fundamental regulations.

As for detailed rules of procedure, it is not surprising to find that the Church, faced more and more frequently with the duty of exercising her judicial power, adopted much from Roman law into ecclesiastical procedure.[14] In the beginning of the seventh century Pope Gregory the Great recognized Roman law as a subsidiary source for directing Ecclesiastical trials. Reviewing the cases of bishops Januarius and Stephanus, St. Gregory declared among other things that priests were to be tried according to the law and canons by their own bishops, and bishops were to be tried by the Metropolitan or Patriarchal See. He frequently quotes from the Theodosian Code and from the Justinian Code and Novels. One pertinent point about the sentence he defines in quoting the Code (7, 44, 3). He prescribed that a sentence which was not drawn up in written form and pronounced from it, was void. For detailed rules of procedure on points not regulated by ecclesiastical law, it was ordered that the rules of the Roman law were to be followed.[15] This seems to be the first official adoption of Roman law procedure in Canon law.

[11] C. 5—Mansi, IV, 438.

[12] Council of Chalcedon (451), (15 session), C. 9—Mansi, VII, 417.

[13] *Nov.* C. 21, CXXIII.

[14] Devoti, *Institutionum Canonicarum,* IV, 1 ff.

[15] *Epist Gregory M.* 45 (603), XIII, Capitulare I et II—*MPL,* 77, 1294.

In regard to the form of the sentence of this period, a few important facts are to be noted. After being drawn up in written form, it was pronounced orally to the parties concerned. If they refused to appear, it was sent to them by messengers. At the beginning of the sentence mention was usually made of the Divine Name in some form or of the name of the Holy Trinity. The thirty-two bishops and twenty-three archimandrites, who subscribed to the sentence of condemnation which they drew up against Eutyches in the Council of Constantinople (448), declared in it, that they with sorrow and regret through Our Lord Jesus Christ removed him from every priestly office and from the communion of the faithful.[16] The dispositive part of the sentence from the Council of Ephesus (431) against Nestorius was given as a pronouncement from Our Lord Jesus Christ declared through the Synod.[17] It was subscribed by the bishops and sent to Nestorius who had refused to appear.

Art. 2. The Pseudo-Isidorian Decretals

In the ninth century there appeared a collection of Canon law known as the Isidorian Decretals. While this collection is for the greater part spurious, some of its canons and decrees are authentic. The compilation was made about 850 A. D.[18] Hinschius holds that it originated in Rheims.[19] Fournier assigns it to the vicinity of Le Mans in the Province of Tours.[20]

In Canon 3 of the Epistle of Eleutherius [21] it is stated that the judge is not to pass sentence until the whole case in question is thoroughly investigated and the truth is established; he is directed to frequently interrogate the witnesses to avoid the chance of passing the truth over unrevealed. According to the Second Epistle of

[16] Mansi, VI, 497.

[17] "Igitur dominus noster Jesus Christus, quem suis ille blasphemus vocibus impetivit, per sanctissimam hanc synodum eumdem Nestorium episcopali dignitate privatum et ab universo sacerdotum consortio et coetu alienum esse definit"—Mansi, IV, 1211.

[18] Hinschius, *Decretales Pseudo-Isidorianae*, p. CCI; Fournier-LaBras, *Histoire des Collections Canoniques en Occident*, I, p. 201.

[19] *Op. cit.*, p. CCXI.

[20] Fournier-LaBras, *op. cit.*, I, p. 201.

[21] Hinschius, *op. cit.*, p. 126.

Evaristus (C. 10-11),[22] the sentence was not to be pronounced in a precipitous fashion to avoid the fallacy of presuming crime rather than waiting to prove it. The motives of vituperators and accusers of bishops and priests were to be investigated to determine if they were prompted by love of God or by vainglory, hatred, malice or cupidity. Canon 4 of the Decrees of Zeppherinus [23] ordained that a sentence was invalid if pronounced in the absence of the defendant. From Canon 4 of the First Epistle of Felix [24] it is found that sentence against a bishop could not be passed unless the crime was confessed or proven by trustworthy witnesses. All of the foregoing canons are spurious.[25]

Art. 3. Legislation from the Decree of Gratian

The Decree of Gratian was written about 1142 A. D. Most of its regulations on the sentence are substantially the same as those in Roman law, from which the greater part directly or indirectly originated. The Decree as a whole, being drawn up by private authority and composed of authentic and spurious canons, has no legislative value; however authentic parts enjoy legal force. It exercised a very profound influence in guiding judicial practice of the time and on subsequent legislation.

The importance of this collection can scarcely be exaggerated. Its publication marks the dawn of the golden age of Canon law, the period from the middle of the twelfth century to about the middle of the fourteenth. It was during this era that the greatest strides were made in the development of the substantive, and especially of the adjective law of the Church. It produced some of the greatest legal minds of all time. To estimate in full its cultural contributions to human society would be a worthy task for competent scholars. It is to be noted that the golden age of Canon law coincides with what some reputable scholars of recent years consider as the true period of the Renaissance. Their view is that the real Renaissance began in the middle of the twelfth century and was definitely Christian, and

[22] Hinschius, *op. cit.*, p. 92.
[23] Hinschius, *op. cit.*, p. 131.
[24] Hinschius, *op. cit.*, p. 198.
[25] Hinschius, *op. cit.*, p. LXXVIII.

that what is commonly considered as the period of the Renaissance was in truth only its period of decadence. Certainly their views find considerable substantiation in the tremendous revival of jurisprudence under the aegis of the Church.

The Decree of Gratian contains considerable legislation on procedure. From this will be quoted some of the relevant matter which seems to have a bearing on the present legislation of the Code on the sentence. Gratian quoting from the Justinian Code states that a definitive sentence which does not contain a condemnation or absolution is null.[26] The rules for the valuation of the testimony of the witnesses by the judge, quote much from the various laws of the Code and Digest; and many have real practical merit.[27]

The Decree declares that before condemnation by sentence in criminal cases one must be convicted by proper testimony or confess.[28] The canon quoted is spurious being attributed to Pope Felix, but quite likely drawn from the Fourth Council of Carthage (C. 28) and the Theodosian Code (9, 40, 1).[29] The sentence was not to be hurriedly pronounced and the judge must wait until facts were open and laid bare.[30] This Canon attributed to Pope Evaristus is apocryphal.[31] The judge should not give the sentence until questionable facts are cleared and the truth is ascertained; a certain sentence is not to be given in a doubtful case.[32] Attributed to Pope Eleutherius (Epistola ad Galliae Provincias), this Canon is spurious, and is evidently from the Theodosian Code.[33] The foregoing regulations Gratian appropriates in substance from the Pseudo-Isidorian Decretals.[34]

An important prescription of the Decree was that the sentence must be drawn up in written form.[35] It is derived from the Epistles of Gregory the Great.[36]

[26] C. 41, C. II, q. 6; *cf. Cod.* 7, 45, 3.

[27] C. 3, C. IV, q. 2 et 3.

[28] C. 5, C. II, q. 1.

[29] Berardi, *Gratiani Canones,* I, pars. 2, C. XXIV.

[30] C. 20, C. II, q. 1.

[31] Berardi, *op. cit.,* I, pars. 2, C. III.

[32] C. 11, C. XXX, q. 5.

[33] Berardi, *op. cit.,* I, pars. 2, C. XI; *cf. Theodosian Code* 2, 18, 1.

[34] *Cf.* Art. 2, The Pseudo-Isidorian Decretals.

[35] C. 7 (n. 14), C. II, q. 1.

[36] *Ep.* 45 (603), XIII—*MPL,* 77, 1294.

ART. 4. DECRETALS OF GREGORY IX

The work of Gratian was soon followed by other collections of Church Law. They were known as *Compilations*. These collections together with the Decree of Gratian contained many imperfections and contradictions. There arose considerable confusion in the study and in the administration of Canon law. To obviate this condition, in 1234 Pope Gregory IX promulgated an authentic collection of Church law. This compilation, known as the *Decretals*, was made by Raymund de Penaforte. Much important legislation on the sentence is to be found in it. The purpose here will be to consider those canons, which indicate notable changes in legislation on the subject or which have had an influence in forming the present regulations of Canon 1868 to 1877 in the Code.

The Decretals declared that when the trial is finished and the defence is heard, the judge should scrutinize all the facts of the case for the purpose of pronouncing the sentence.[37] The judge was to study all the evidence, depositions, confessions, allegations, and all other proofs presented, and then make up his mind (formet motum animi sui).[38] The sentence must conform to the law and legitimate custom; if it is opposed to certain and evident ecclesiastical laws or legitimate customs, it is not valid.[39] If it contained a manifest injustice, it was not to be upheld; but if it did not evidently and notoriously offend against the right of a litigant, it was normally to be considered valid until appealed. The appeal was to be made within ten days.[40]

A very important statute of this collection of law was that the controversies of the litigants be terminated quickly but with due precaution being observed of preserving justice and correctness.[41] Another statute directed that the decisive part of the sentence should

[37] C. 10, X, *de fide instr.*, II, 22.

[38] C. 6, X, *de renunciatione*, I, 9; c. 27, X, *de testibus et attestationibus*, II, 20; *cf.* Wernz-Vidal, *De Processibus*, n. 586.

[39] C. 1 et 3, X, *de sent. et re iud.*, II, 27.

[40] C. 3 et 13, X, *de sent. et re iud.*, II, 27; *D.* 49, 1, 19; *cf.* Wernz-Vidal, *op. cit.*, n. 592.

[41] C. 2, X, *de sent. et re iud.*, II, 27.

be given in definite terms, and it should be understood as the judge willed and intended.[42]

The meaning of *res iudicata* in the Canon law of this time is to be noted. The definition quoted here is that of Ferraris, a summation from the Decretals.[43] "Res autem iudicata proprie sumpta dicitur sententia, quae post lapsum decem dierum accepit auctoritatem et vires rei iudicatae; adeo ut pro veritate accipiatur, et postea retractari non possit, et quicumque velit contradicere, non audiatur." [44] This differs from the definition of Roman law.[45] The Decretals ordained an important exception to this rule in matrimonial causes, which were never to attain the status of *res iudicata* and were to be recalled whenever error was proven.[46]

That the provisions of civil law might be helpful at times to the judge in coming to a decision, seems to be recognized in this time. In one place it is prescribed that the judge, circumspect and conversant in precautions of civil law, forms his own conscientious opinion from testimony and arguments which appear to be very reliable.[47]

Some prudent regulations on the valuation of testimony are enacted in the Decretals. One practical instance will be mentioned. It is declared that when witnesses contradict one another, their evidence is not to be thrown out, but credence is to be given accordingly as persons are more trustworthy and better qualified, as their evidence is more likely to be true, and also in accordance to the agreement of the greater numbers; but numbers yield to fewer and better qualified witnesses.[48]

The Decretals made provisions that a civil sentence and the sentence of an incompetent judge are void. It was enacted that clerics, who either confessed a crime before a secular judge or were convicted by him, are not thereby to be condemned by the Ordinary.

[42] C. 15, X, *de verborum significatione,* V, 40.

[43] C. 13, X, *de sent. et re iud.*, II, 27.

[44] Ferraris, *Bibliotheca,* art., "Sententia," n. 41.

[45] *D.* 42, 1, 1.

[46] C. 7, X, *de sent. et re iud.*, II, 27.

[47] C. 27, X, *de testibus et attestationibus,* II, 20.

[48] C. 32, X, *de testibus et attestationibus,* II, 20.

Such a sentence or confession, where it is not one's proper judge, does not hold before the ecclesiastical court.[49]

On the motivation of the sentence, the law of this time was quite similar to Roman law which insisted that the sentence be determinate, but did not insist that it be motivated.[50] Hence it was not necessary that the reasons *in facto* and *in iure,* upon which the disposition of the sentence was based, should be enumerated.

> Quum autem in plerisque locis, in quibus copia prudentum habetur, id moris existat, quod omnia, quae iudicem movent, non exprimantur in sententiis proferendis, vobis taliter respondemus, quod, quum ex depositionibus testium praedictorum constiterit vobis, sententiam a iudice suo fuisse prolatam, propter auctoritatem iudiciariam praesumi debet, omnia legitime processisse.[51]

In observing the canons on the sentence the judges were obliged by the general rule which applied to the whole process that the canons governing ecclesiastical judgments were to be followed, not according to the judges' own opinions, but according to the proper authoritative meaning of them.[52]

Art. 5. *Liber Sextus*

The next important source to be considered is the *Liber Sextus.* Pope Boniface VIII ordered this collection as an addition to the Decretals. Many provisions touching on the sentence are found in it. Several points relevant to this subject deserve mention. One or two regulations have particularly had important bearing on subsequent legislation.

Real merit is to be found in an instruction to the judge for making his decision. The *Liber Sextus* prescribes that in all particulars of ecclesiastical procedure, especially in determining and pronouncing the sentence, the judges should hold before their eyes the Al-

[49] C. 4, X, *de iudiciis,* II, 1.

[50] *D.* 42, 1, 59; c. 6, X, *de renuntiatione,* I, 9; *cf.* Wernz-Vidal, *op. cit.,* n. 592.

[51] C. 16, X, *de sent. et re iud.,* II, 27.

[52] C. 1, X, *de constitutionibus,* I, 2.

mighty Creator that they may judge as if according to His Will. It admonishes them not to vindicate personal malice, nor to show partiality, never to yield to fear, nor to act in hope of being rewarded; all of which tend to subvert justice. One who offends against justice or acts against the dictates of his conscience, either by being over-indulgent, or by being base, is to be punished by suspension.[53]

In cases where moral certitude was not established and the rights of the parties were undetermined, the general principle of favoring the defendant rather than the plaintiff held.[54]

An important statute was enacted on the question of motivation in the sentence. It demanded that in cases of excommunication, the sentence is to contain the sustaining motives. Anyone inflicting excommunication gives it in writing and states the reasons.[55] This statute indicates a trend which will in subsequent legislation be made more extensive.

On the publication of the sentence, the *Liber Sextus* rules that in collegiate tribunals one of the judges, with the others present and approving, reads the sentence which was in writing; it is given as pronounced by all and therefore spoken in the plural number.[56] In the ordinary tribunal, only the *proper judge* could give a valid sentence; it was to be *in writing,* and was *pronounced* by the judge *seated.* These provisions obliged under pain of nullity.[57]

Art. 6. The Sentence in the Summary Process

The constitution *"Saepe"* of Pope Clement V on the summary process, insisting on the fundamental regulations of formal trial, but omitting many of its solemnities, allowed the following method of publication of the sentence: The parties were cited, but not by a peremptory order, to appear, and the definitive sentence, determined according as it should be from the petitions, proofs, and acts of the

[53] C. 1, *de sent. et re iud.*, II, 14, in VI°.

[54] Reg. 11, *R. I.* in VI°.

[55] C. 1, *de verborum significatione,* V, 11, in VI°.

[56] C. 4, *de sent. et re iud.*, II, 14, in VI°.

[57] C. 5, *de sent. et re iud.*, II, 14 in VI°; *cf.* Vermeersch-Creusen, *op. cit.*, III, n. 233.

case and drawn up in writing, was pronounced by the judge either seated or standing.[58]

Art. 7. Regulations of the Council of Trent

Two very important legislative enactments on the sentence were made in the Council of Trent. In Session 24, *de reformatione*, cap. 20, it was enacted that all cases of the ecclesiastical forum are to be terminated in the first instance within two years from filing suit or charges. " . . . omnino saltem infra biennium a die motae terminentur." [59] Previous to this the Roman law [60] which admitted three years for civil cases and two years for criminal cases, was generally followed; but in particular cases where justice demanded it, time was extended.[61]

The other enactment ordained that no appeal from interlocutory sentences was to be admitted except in three cases. Appeal was to be allowed in cases where interlocutory sentences had definitive force, or where they caused damage otherwise irreparable.[62] Likewise appeal was to be admitted in cases where no appeal of the definitive sentence was allowed.[63]

Art. 8. Legislation After the Council of Trent

It is desired to note legislation of this period which effected vital change in or has some practical relation to the present prescription of the Code.

The most important legislation affecting the sentence during this period is to be found in the constitution of Pope Benedict XIV, "*Dei Miseratione.*" [64] This constitution prescribes the procedure to be

[58] C. 2, *de verborum significatione*, V, 11, in Clem.; *cf.* Lega, *De Iudiciis Ecclesiasticis*, I, n. 596.

[59] Mansi, XXXIII, 168.

[60] *Cod.* 3, 1, 13.

[61] Ferraris, *op. cit.*, art. "Sententia," n. 37 ff.

[62] Session 24, *de reformatione*, cap. 20—Mansi XXXIII, 168.

[63] Session 13, *de reformatione*, cap. 1—Mansi, XXXIII, 86; Ferraris, *op. cit.*, art. "Sententia," n. 33 ff.; art. "Appellatio," n. 24 ff.

[64] 3 nov. 1741—*Fontes*, n. 318.

observed in matrimonial causes. Abuses had developed in trying these causes, and to eliminate them Benedict XIV laid down new laws of procedure. These laws are the basis of our present procedure in matrimonial causes. The constitution obliged every bishop to appoint to his diocese a defender of the bond (*Matrimoniorum Defensor*), who was required to take part in all matrimonial trials.[65] If the defender of the bond was not legitimately cited or notified for the trial, the sentence would be invalid because all the acts were nullified.[66] He was obliged to appeal a sentence for nullity given for the first time in any instance when the interested party failed to appeal. From the second sentence for nullity the defender was to appeal when he was not satisfied in his conscience with the sentence.[67] Another vital prescription enacted was the requirement of two conformable sentences being passed before either of the parties could enter a new union.

> . . . nisi duo iudicata, vel resolutiones, aut sententiae penitus similes, et conformes, a quibus neque pars, neque, defensor matrimonii crediderit appellandum, emanaverint.[68]

The conformity required here was more than mere conformity in the declaration of the nullity of the marriage. "Penitus similes et conformes" demands beyond concordance in the disposition that the motive or cause, upon which the marriage was declared null, is the same in both instances.[69]

An instruction given in 1840, following the prescriptions of the constitution *"Dei Miseratione,"* declared that in matrimonial causes the sentence was to be given after the final hearing was concluded and the defender of the bond (*defensor matrimonii*) felt no need of further hearing. If the sentence declared for nullity of matrimony, then the defender of the bond was to appeal the case; because in case of declarations of nullity two conformable sentences were required.[70]

[65] Const., *"Dei Miseratione,"* n. 5, 6. A vestige of a similar court official is found before this. *Cf.* Hostiensis, *Summa Aurea,* IV, p. 322.

[66] Const., *"Dei Miseratione,"* n. 7.

[67] Const., *"Dei Miseratione,"* n. 8-11.

[68] Const., *"Dei Miseratione,"* n. 14.

[69] *Cf.* Cappello, *op. cit.,* III, n. 887.

[70] S. C. C. instr., 22 aug. 1840—*Collectanea,* n. 911.

In criminal causes the sentence was to be given after all the evidence was heard, the fiscal procurator (*procurator fiscalis*) had concluded, and the final defense had been given. In case of condemnation (*damnationis*), it was to contain explicitly the canonical sanction inflicted upon the defendant.[71]

During this period the practice of motivating the sentence was being insisted upon in various instances. Thus the instruction to the bishops of the United States prescribed that the sentence was to be drawn up in writing and the reasons upon which it was based were to be stated succinctly with nothing essential left out. It was to be signed by the judge and secretary, and stamped with the seal of the episcopal curia. The bailiff (*apparitor*) notified the parties and a copy of it was given to them.[72]

In appraising the force of evidence upon which the sentence is to be based, there are several pertinent regulations. The constitution *"Intolerabilis"* admitted in certain cases (corrupt and unlawful practices referring to benefices), where it was difficult to prove crime, some presumptions and conjectures as legitimate proof; these presumptions and conjectures sustained by witnesses were given force of full proof.[73] The constitution *"Universi"* declared along the same lines that: to avoid pernicious crime (solicitation) going unpunished because of difficulty of proof, the Inquisitors were granted faculties, in cases where witness concurred with indications and presumptions to sustain guilt, of declaring condemnation according to their own judgment in the matter.[74] From the context of these two constitutions it is evident that the proof had to be such as to convince the judge with moral certainty of the guilt of the persons. This is explicitly reiterated in other precepts given for directing the judge in forming his opinion; of which precepts it is pertinent to mention that contained in the instruction of the S. C. Ep. et Reg., 11 iun. 1880, n. 16.[75] Herein it is stated that to establish the fact of crime is the function of legal proof, which should evince truth or at least give

[71] S. C. Ep. et Reg., instr. 11 iun. 1880, n. 35—*Fontes*, n. 2005.

[72] S. C. de Prop. Fide, instr., a. 1883, n. 24—*Collectanea*, n. 1587.

[73] S. Pius V, const. *"Intolerabilis,"* 1 iun. 1569, nn. 4, 6—*Fontes*, n. 130.

[74] Gregory XV, const., *"Universi,"* 30 aug., 1622, n. 5—*Fontes*, n. 201.

[75] *Fontes*, n. 2005.

moral certitude removing any reasonable doubt to the contrary. In another instruction on criminal and disciplinary cases, is to be found a close paraphrase of the instruction immediately above.[76]

The instruction on matrimonial cases to the bishops of this country throws an interesting light on the question of establishing the trustworthiness of the witnesses. It prescribes that, concerning all who were called or are to be called, the moderator (*moderator actorum*) shall inquire about their integrity and truthfulness from their pastors or from other reliable persons. These testimonial letters may be shown, and if so, are to be inscribed in the acts of the case.[77]

Art. 9. Processual Rules for the Roman Tribunals

When Pius X [78] reorganized the Roman Curia, he enacted the laws of procedure for the Roman tribunals in the "Lex propria S. R. Rotae et Signaturae Apostolicae." [79] These were supplemented at different times by subsequent legislation. First the procedural rules for the Rota were made more complete in the "Regulae servandae in iudiciis apud S. R. Rotae Tribunal." [80] Later there appeared the corresponding regulations for procedure in the Signatura in the "Regulae servandae in iudiciis apud Supremum Signaturae Apostolicae Tribunal." [81] A supplement to the regulations for the Signatura is found in the "Appendix, Ad Regulas Servandas in iudiciis apud Supremum Signaturae Apostolicae Tribunal." [82] The provisions of procedure on the sentence found in these groups of procedural regulations for the Roman tribunals are so similar to those found in the Code that they seem proper to the commentary to be taken up on the prescriptions of the Code, and therefore, will be treated in the second part of this work. Suffice it to say that these sets of procedural laws on the sentence are the immediate source of the laws laid down in the Code.

[76] S. C. de Prop. Fide, instr. a., 1883, n. XVI—*Collectanea*, n. 1586.

[77] S. C. de Prop. de Fide, instr., a. 1883, n. 16—*Collectanea*, n. 1587.

[78] Const. *"Sapienti Consilio,"* 29 iun. 1908—*Fontes*, n. 682.

[79] 29 iun. 1908—*ASS*, XLI (1908), 440.

[80] 4 aug. 1910—*AAS*, (1910), 783.

[81] 6 mart. 1912—*AAS*, IV (1912), 187.

[82] 3 nov. 1915.

It is important to keep in mind that since the Code the Roman tribunals are to observe the prescriptions of the Code in their procedure.[83] Any laws of these regulations for the Roman tribunals, which are contrary to the Code, are abrogated.[84] On the other hand, where there is no contradiction, the regulations of the Roman tribunal may often be helpful in interpreting the provisions of the Code.[85]

Art. 10. Conclusion

To sum up what has been stated in this historical synopsis, a few facts will suffice to indicate a general outline. The ecclesiastical sentence traces in substance its origin to the sentence in Roman law. The term was first applied to the solution offered by private arbitrators to settle controversies amongst the Romans. Later it was given legal status and it became the official pronouncement to settle disputes and facts in the administration of the judicial power of Roman government. The nature of the sentence and many of its legal requirements as found in Roman law were incorporated into Canon law and served as the basis of ecclesiastical regulations. In the procedure of the Church there has been a development of the prescription on the sentence which served on one hand to establish safeguards for equity and justice and on the other to give efficient administration of ecclesiastical law according to changing conditions in the expansion of the Church. Evidence of this is indicated in the tendency of later legislation towards motivating the sentence, in the institution of the defender of the bond into the matrimonial trial, in the insistence upon moral certitude for a decision, and in the canonical notion of the *res iudicata*. The present day legislation on the sentence will be discussed in detail in the following part of this work.

[83] Canon 1555, § 2.

[84] Canon 6, n. 1; *cf.* Roberti, *op. cit.*, n. 136.

[85] Canon 6, nn. 2, 3, 4.

CHAPTER IV

SUPPLEMENTARY COMMENTARY ON CANON 1868

Canon 1868, § 1. Legitima pronuntiatio qua iudex causam a litigantibus propositam et iudiciali modo pertractatam definit, sententia est: eaque *interlocutoria* dicitur, si dirimit incidentem causam; *definitiva*, si principalem.

§ 2. Ceterae iudicis pronuntiationes *decreta* vocantur.

The definition and exposition of the terms contained in this canon together with some commentary have been given in Chapter I. There remain to be emphasized several requisites of the sentence and decrees as well as some additional points of commentary.

Art. 1. Prime Requisites of the Sentence

§ 1. *Jurisdiction and Competency*

The first requirement for passing sentence is that the tribunal must be competent, since only a competent judge can pass a valid sentence. This makes it necessary that the tribunal has: first, the power of giving judgment in the abstract—(jurisdiction); and, seconly, it must have title to do in a particular cause—(competency).[1] In the diocesan tribunal a legitimate pronouncement must, therefore, come under one of the titles of competency determined and enumerated in the Code by Canons 1560 to 1568.[2] In case of absolute incompetency [3] the sentence is entirely void so as to admit of no remedy (*insanabilis*).[4] In cases of relative incompetency prorogation may be admitted under certain conditions, and the sentence is valid.[5]

[1] Wernz-Vidal, *De Processibus,* n. 46; Roberti, *De Processibus,* n. 54.

[2] Canon 1559.

[3] Canons 1556, 1557.

[4] Canon 1892, § 1.

[5] Wernz-Vidal, *op. cit.,* n. 63; Roberti, *op. cit.,* n. 55.

This is not the free prorogation of forum [6] admitted previous to the Code, and since abolished.[7] But rather is it such that it prorogues competency when the parties do not make exception according to Canon 1628, § 1, and the judge does not advert to or recognize his relative incompetence. Besides this case, the defect of competency is supplied by law [8] in common error and in cases of doubt.[9] Otherwise the principle that a sentence *a non suo iudice non tenet* [10] holds. Recourse against the sentence of a relatively incompetent judge is only by way of appeal.[11] In absolute incompetency, recourse is *per querelam nullitatis*.[12] In a collegiate tribunal, if one judge is incompetent or fails to act, he is to be replaced before a valid sentence can be passed.[13]

§ 2. *Right of Parties to Stand in Court*

The juridic standing of the parties before the court is an important item to be ascertained before passing sentence. A valid sentence can not be pronounced in a cause where one of the parties has no juridic standing in court. The sentence in such a case would be irremediably invalid.[14] Ecclesiastical personality is based on baptism.[15] The prescriptions on juridic capacity are found in Canons 1646 to 1654. Juridic incapacity may be relative or absolute. In absolute incapacity, an absolute substitute is required, *e. g.*, for minors and insane persons. In relative incapacity, a procurator should act for the parties. Excommunicated persons are prohibited to act, rather than incapacitated.[16]

[6] C. 18, X, *de foro competenti,* II, 2.

[7] Canon 1559.

[8] Canon 209.

[9] Wernz-Vidal, *op. cit.*, n. 63; Roberti, *op. cit.*, n. 56.

[10] C. 4, X, *de foro competenti,* II, 2.

[11] Eichmann, *Das Prozessrecht des Codex Iuris Canonici,* p. 172.

[12] Canon 1892.

[13] *Cf.* Canon 207, § 3.

[14] Canon 1892, n. 2.

[15] Canon 87.

[16] Roberti, *op. cit.*, n. 196; *cf.* Noval, *op. cit.*, n. 250.

§ 3. *Status of Non-Catholics*

Non-Catholics have no juridic standing in ecclesiastical courts in accord with Canon 87 and the declaration of the Holy Office.[17] This declaration stated that they cannot assume the part of *actor* or petitioner in a trial except when they are admitted by the Holy Office. While the declaration of the Holy Office only explicitly mentions matrimonial causes, Roberti [18] holds that it applies to all causes. Infidels have no ecclesiastical personality. Baptized non-Catholics have an *obex* to the exercise of the rights of baptized persons. They are not considered simply excommunicated, and therefore they lack even the rights of this class;[19] they are *ipso facto infames,*[20] or at least presumed such,[21] for having joined a non-Catholic sect or for having publicly adhered to it, and therefore they are incapacitated.[22] Moreover to admit at random non-Catholics as petitioners would be to invite contempt of judicial authority in ecclesiastical procedure.[23]

The force of this prohibition against non-Catholics is indicated by some recent rescripts which were sent to the Bishop of Berlin. The following case was presented to the Holy Office. A Catholic, living illicitly with a non-Catholic previously married to another non-Catholic, denounced the marriage of the non-Catholics to the Ordinary. The question was asked whether the Ordinary or promoter of justice could institute action against the marriage. The Holy Office replied that recourse was to be had to the Holy Office in each case.[24] A similar declaration is found in a rescript from the Sacred Congregation of the Sacraments. The question proposed in this case was whether the Ordinary or promoter of justice, after the denunciation

[17] S. C. S. Off., 27 ian. 1928—*AAS,* XX (1928), 75.

[18] *Apollinaris,* I (1928), 217.

[19] Canon 1653, § 1, allows excommunicated persons to act through a procurator in spiritual causes; Canon 1628, § 3 allows them to take exception to the excommunication.

[20] Canon 2314, § 1, n. 3.

[21] Canon 2200, § 2.

[22] Canon 2294, § 1.

[23] *Apollinaris,* I (1928), 216; *Il Mon Eccl.,* XL (1928), 66-69.

[24] 30 nov. 1931—*AKKR,* CXII (1932), 154.

of the nullity of a marriage according to Canon 1971, § 2, had the right of instituting action, or if the permission of the Holy See was needed. The response was that the permission of the Holy See was not required except in causes which were reserved to the Holy Office by its decree of January 27, 1928.[25] These rescripts indicate that no marriage causes concerning two non-Catholics (baptized or not baptized) are to be brought into court for formal trial without having recourse to the Holy Office.

The exception made under Canon 1990 will be treated under the documentary process.

§ 4. *Power of an Auditor*

Since it frequently happens that an auditor is employed in a trial, it is well to define the limitations on his power to pass sentence. For the most part his powers will depend upon the mandate of appointment with the limitations contained therein or determined by custom.[26] The law proscribes the passing of a definitive sentence by the auditor;[27] which proscription evidently includes a prejudicial interlocutory sentence, *i. e.*, one having definitive force. He cannot terminate the trial in another manner, *e. g.*, by compromise, by agreement, etc.[28] However, he may decide incidental questions by a decree or an interlocutory sentence which is not prejudicial. The auditor signs the decree or sentence together with the notary. Recourse against these is to be had to the judge who made the appointment, since the power of the auditor is dependent upon the will of the delegating judge.[29]

§ 5. *A Sentence Must Be Just*

The underlying philosophy of canonical jurisprudence in applying the law by judicial process is found in the requisite that the sentence must be just. This means that the sentence must be evolved only

[25] 3 nov. 1931—*AKKR*, CXII (1932), 155.
[26] Lega, *De Iudiciis Ecclesiasticis*, I, n. 146.
[27] Canon 1582.
[28] Noval, *op cit.*, n. 135.
[29] Roberti, *op. cit.*, n. 110.

according to the prescriptions of law. When the sentence has some substantial deficiency contrary to the law, it is invalid and unjust; when deficient in accidental matters, it is valid but unjust.[30] Hence a sentence manifestly contrary to certain and clear laws or legitimately prescribed customs (*contra ius constitutionis*) is invalid, and is subject to recourse *per querelam nullitatis*. This same holds true, if the sentence offends evidently and notoriously against the rights of a litigant (*contra ius litigatoris*); however, in this case unless the injustice is notorious, the presumption favors the action of the judge and the sentence is considered valid until appealed.[31]

§ 6. *Conformity to "Libellus"*

Conformity of the sentence to the *libellus* or petition is required.[32] This quality is supposed by the prescriptions[33] of the Code. The conformity is threefold: *in re*, so that the judge is not to pronounce on another matter which is not petitioned; *in causa petendi*, so that the judge is not to inject another cause as the basis of the petition; *in actione*, so that the judge is not to substitute another action for the one instituted by the petitioner.[34] Hence in a case where a judicial petition [35] is presented, the judge cannot *ex officio* substitute a criminal denunciation [36] and pass sentence on this cause. The sentence would be invalid, and it admits of recourse *per querelam nullitatis*. For instance, the Ordinary commits to the tribunal for decision a petition presented by Caia for separation *a marito ob eius vitam ignominiosam*; the judge cannot *ex officio* inspect for crime (*ex adulterio*) and grant a separation on that ground. The sentence would be null.[37]

[30] Coronata, *Institutiones Iuris Canonici*, n. 1394.

[31] Cc. 3, 13, X, *de sent. et re iud.*, II, 27; *cf.* Lega, *op. cit.*, I, n. 606; Schmalzgrueber, *Ius Ecclesiasticum*, II, t. 27, n. 42; Reiffenstuel, *Ius Canonicum*, II, t. 27, n. 70; Wernz-Vidal, *op. cit.*, n. 592.

[32] C. 6, X, *de iudiciis*, II, 1; c. 2, *de verborum significatione*, V, 11.

[33] Canon 1873; *cf.* Cappello, *De Sacramentis*, III, n. 887.

[34] Schmalzgrueber, *op. cit.*, II, t. 5, nn. 1, 4, 31; Pirhing, *Ius Canonicum*, II, 27, n. 32 ff.; Wernz-Vidal, *op. cit.*, n. 592.

[35] Canon 1706 ff.

[36] Canon 1936 ff.

[37] *Apollinaris*, II (1929), 76, 77.

To safeguard public good when involved, the judge has a duty to inspect thoroughly a cause in every way, and if necessary, to order a change in the *libellus, i. e.*, substitute the objective, cause or action. If, in a matrimonial cause based on one cause (*e. g., vis et metus*) there develops as the basis of the action another cause (*e. g., impotentia*), the judge is not petitioned for a change in the *libellus*, he is *ex officio* to order the change. Criminal charges can be interjected only by the promoter of justice. Criminal denunciation is to be made to the Ordinary [38] by the parties or by the judge if necessary.[39] An occult crime revealed during a trial is not liable to prosecution.[40]

To conclude succinctly, the sentence should conform to the *libellus* in the objective sought, the cause proposed and the action instituted.

Art. 2. Use and Form of Decrees

Some further commentary on decrees as to their use and form is necessary to supplement that given previously.[41] Whether an incidental question is to be settled by a decree or an interlocutory sentence is left to the discretion of the judge according to the gravity and quality of the matter.[42] Important questions are usually to be decided by an interlocutory sentence. Prejudicial questions and absolutory decisions *ab observatione iudicii,* when contested by one of the parties, ought always to be determined by a sentence after the due judicial argumentation; and should the judge use a decree, appeal is allowed against it because it is objectively a sentence of definitive force.[43] A sentence *ab observatione iudicii* is not properly definitive, since it only *hic et nunc* relieves the defendant from the instance and not from the action of the *actor,* and hence, does not pass into *rem iudicatam.*[44]

[38] Canon 1936.
[39] Canon 1935.
[40] *Apollinaris,* II (1929), 76, 77.
[41] Chapter I.
[42] Canon 1840, § 1.
[43] Coronata, *op. cit.*, n. 1394; Roberti, *op. cit.*, n. 446.
[44] Eichmann, *Lehrbuch des katholischen Kirchenrechts,* p. 579, note 6.

As to form, decrees should be issued under the heading "Decretum." Then follows the name of the judge or judges with the statement of the question, adding whether they were given *ex officio* or at the instance of the parties. After this, follows the disposition of the issue. *Decreta decisoria* should have the reasons of law and fact stated before the disposition. It is concluded with the date and place, if not stated already, and the signature of the judge or judges and the notary.[45]

[45] Roberti, *op. cit.*, n. 188.

CHAPTER V

THE DECISIVE FACTOR IN THE SENTENCE—MORAL CERTITUDE (CANON 1869)

Canon 1869, § 1. Ad pronuntiationem cuiuslibet sententiae requiritur in iudicis animo moralis certitudo circa rem sententia definiendam.

§ 2. Hanc certitudinem iudex haurire debet ex actis et probatis.

§ 3. Probationes autem aestimare iudex ex sua conscientia, nisi lex aliquid expresse statuat de efficacia alicuius probationis.

§ 4. Iudex qui eam certitudinem efformare sibi non potuit, pronuntiet non constare de iure actoris et reum dimittat, nisi agatur de causa favorabili, quo in casu pro ipsa pronuntiandum est, et salvo praescripto Can. 1697, § 2.

Justice will not prevail in the sentence if irrelevant factors or the whims or prejudices of the judge enter into the solution of a cause. Therefore Canon 1869 definitely determines that judgment must be passed according to those principles, which from the standpoint of jurisprudence, are unassailable. Canon 1869 defines the fundamental decisive factor in determining a sentence as moral certitude; which principle is established in all human law. Moral certitude will be treated under five articles: definition, its basis, its motives, the solution of doubts, and the question of the private knowledge of the judge.

Art. 1. Definition

Certitude may be defined in a generic sense as the stable adherence of the mind to some proposition without fear of error. This allows three classifications dependent upon the possibility or probability of error: metaphysical, physical, and moral. Metaphysical certitude excludes all possibility of error, as in the certainty of first principles and the immediate conclusions thereof. Physical certitude excludes the possibility of error according to natural laws, and is subject to exception only by divine intervention, *i. e.*, by a miracle. Moral certitude excludes the fear of error according to the law of the habits and inclinations of men in ordinary circumstances; thus it is certain that a mother would not give her child poison.[1] From the nature of the judicial process, the last mentioned is the only form of certitude required.

Canon 1869, § 1, prescribes that there must exist in the mind of the judge moral certitude about the matter to be defined in the sentence. This certitude excludes the probability but not the possibility of error. Since the degree of probability may vary, it is necessary to distinguish two kinds of moral certitude: perfect and imperfect. Perfect moral certitude excludes all fear of error. Imperfect excludes not all fear of error but only every prudent doubt or grave fear of error. This latter certitude is the one required by law, and as such is recognized to suffice by common sense.[2] St. Thomas[3] declares that "in actibus humanis . . . sufficit probabilis certitudo quae ut in pluribus veritatem attingat, etsi in paucioribus a veritate deficiat." The Angelic Doctor also demonstrates that from a practical viewpoint perfect moral certitude is out of the question:

> Materia moralis talis est quod non est ei conveniens perfecta certitudo.[4]
>
> Certitudo non est similiter quaerenda in omnibus, sed in unaquaque materia secundum proprium modum. Quia vero materia prudentiae sunt singularia contingentia, circa quae sunt operationes humanae, non potest certitudo prudentiae tanta esse, quod omnino sollicitudo tollatur.[5]

In practice therefore a judge observes the precepts of canon law and follows the dictates of justice when, prompted by a moral cer-

[1] Aertnys-Damen, *Theologia Moralis,* I, n. 61.

[2] *Cf.* Noval, *op. cit.*, n. 621; Roberti, *op. cit.*, nn. 324, 448.

[3] *Summa Theologica,* II-II, q. LXX, Art. 2.

[4] *Ethic,* I, lect. 3.

[5] *Summa Theologica,* II-II, q. XLVII, Art. IX, ad 2.

tainty which excludes every prudent doubt and all grave fear of error, he makes his decision. It is not necessary that every misgiving or suspicion of error be resolved before deciding a cause. Such would be humanly impossible. It would lead to interminable perplexities. The judge would be involved in a maze of scruples; the process of law would be paralyzed; but few cases could be satisfactorily completed, and human rights would be left unvindicated.[6]

ART. 2. BASIS OF CERTITUDE

While moral certitude is a necessary requisite in deciding the sentence, it is equally necessary that this certitude be based on an indisputable principle of legal justice: that the mind of the judge is open only to the acts and proofs of the cause being heard. Knowledge from any source not uncovered in the process is no knowledge in a juridic sense. The old legal axiom "quod non est in actis, non est in mundo" must ever be respected. Canon 1869, § 2, expressly legislates that the requisite certitude is to be derived *ex actis et probatis* of the cause. In the light of the old law, the binding force of this prescription becomes even more evident.[7] It applies to all causes, contentious and criminal.

Noval [8] defines the meaning of the terms *ex actis at probatis*. *Ex actis* as: from the assertions and denials, the charges and countercharges, and petitions and defenses evolved in the course of the trial and recorded in the *acta*. These matters may be proposed by the parties in contentious causes, by the judge in causes involving public weal, by the promoter of justice or defendant in criminal causes, by the defender of the bond in matrimonial causes. *Ex probatis* as: from the proofs established by documents, by depositions of witnesses, and by other arguments which were introduced in the trial and recorded in the *acta*.

Obviously the above enumerations are not intended as *taxative*, but rather to indicate in a practical way what is included under *ex*

[6] *Cf.* Lyons, *The Collegiate Tribunal of First Instance*, p. 63.

[7] C. 5, C. II, q. 1; c. 20, C. II, q. 1; c. 10, X, *de fide instr.*, II, 22; c. 6, X, *de renunciatione*, I, 9; c. 27, X, *de testibus et attestationibus*, II, 20.

[8] *Op. cit.*, n. 622.

actis et probatis. The terms include everything done, every act revealed, every legal form of proof presented in the trial, *i. e., acta causae et acta processus.*

The judge therefore is constrained by Canon 1869, § 2, to be guided only by the facts and proofs established in the trial. The prescription is exclusive, prohibiting the admission of any outside information, evidence or fact as a factor to affect the judicial deliberation. The judge in a cause is not acting as a private person but only as a public person in an official capacity. In passing sentence he has before him solely the legal aspect of a public authority applying the law to an individual case according to its merits as revealed in the court procedure.[9] Hence, the moral certitude required in the mind of the judge before determining the sentence must arise, abstracting from all extraneous facts, circumstances or information, solely from the facts and evidence presented in the cause itself.

Art. 3. Question of the Use of Private Knowledge By the Judge

§ 1. *The Three Opinions*

From the foregoing, the tenor of the law seems to be most explicit about the exclusion of private knowledge of the judge from his deliberation on the sentence. However the question has been raised as to whether it applies absolutely to all possible cases. It will be necessary therefore to go into this question at length and treat the three general opinions in this regard. The question is concerned only with cases where there is conflict between the certain personal or private knowledge of the judge and the seemingly conclusive evidence produced in the trial.

The first opinion is that absolutely and universally the judge is bound to follow the evidence established in the trial to the exclusion of any personal knowledge to the contrary. This opinion is supported by St. Thomas[10] as follows:

[9] Bouix, *De Iudiciis Ecclesiasticis,* I, p. 140; Lega, *op. cit.,* I, n. 88; Roberti, *op. cit.,* n. 448; Noval, *op. cit.,* n. 622.

[10] *Summa Theologica,* II-II, q. LXII, Art. 2.

> Iudicare pertinet ad judicem secundum quod fungitur publica potestate; et ideo informari debet in iudicando non secundum id quod ipse novit tanquam privata persona, sed secundum id quod sibi innotescit tanquam personae publicae. Hoc autem innotescit ei et in communi et in particulari: in communi quidem per leges publicas, vel divinas vel humanas, contra quas nullas probationes admittere debet: in particulari autem negotio aliquo per instrumenta et testes, et alia huiusmodi legitima documenta, quae debet sequi in iudicando magis quam id quod ipse novit tanquam privata persona. Ex quo tamen ad hoc adiuvari potest ut districtius discutiat probationes inductas, ut possit earum defectum investigare. Quod si eas non possit de iure repellere, debet, sicut dictum est hic supra, eas in iudicando sequi.

St. Thomas [11] follows the principle even to the infliction of the death penalty upon a person whom the judge knows to be certainly innocent, when the judge cannot turn the case over to another judge or otherwise avoid passing sentence.

The second opinion holds the contrary to the first and declares that the judge is not an automaton to be guided by falsity, and therefore he should never act against his private conscience, but rather he should ignore the *acta et probata* to define the truth from his own personal certitude. This opinion is held by Schmier.[12]

The third opinion proposed by Lessius,[13] distinguishes between civil and minor criminal causes on one hand and major criminal causes on the other, holding that a judge should not inflict a penalty of death in these cases, as an innocent man's right to live supersedes every exigency of public good. Lessius [14] considers it intrinsically evil to condemn to death a person whom the judge knows privately to be innocent; and as an alternative to freeing the person, the judge may refuse to pass judgment. In the civil and minor criminal causes, because of public good, the judge should be guided by the *acta et probata*.

The second opinion may be summarily dismissed because it is universally reproved. Authors unanimously hold that a judge can-

[11] *Op. cit.*, II-II, q. LXIV, Art. 6, ad 3.

[12] *Ius Canonicum Universum,* II, t. I, c. 2, n. 35.

[13] *De Iustitia et Iure,* II, c. 29, d. X, n. 77 ff.

[14] *Op. cit.*, II, c. 29, d. X, nn. 18, 78.

not use his private knowledge to condemn the defendant when the case is not proven against him because of the force of the legal axiom —"actore non probante, reus absolvitur." [15]

The third opinion is recognized as a probable opinion. St. Alphonsus [16] considers Lessius' opinion to be very probable and the condemnation to death of one, whom the judge knows to be innocent, to be intrinsically evil. Vidal [17] holds that in serious criminal causes the judge cannot and ought not condemn by sentence one, whom he knows by private knowledge certainly to be guiltless. Among authors supporting Lessius are to be found Reiffenstuel [18] and Pirhing.[19] As far as the penalty of death or grave bodily punishment is concerned, this opinion is impractical because an ecclesiastical judge is never required to inflict such penalties.

The first opinion seems to be more conformable to the prescriptions of the Code, and it is supported by very cogent arguments. To allow the use of private knowledge in disregard of the proofs presented would undermine the confidence of people in justice from the law. It would impair the usefulness of the courts, and tend to subvert all judicial order. The decisions of judges would be received with suspicion, and few would ever reconcile themselves to unfavorable decisions. For these reasons together with the position of the judge as a public person judging *ex actis et probatis,* Noval [20] considers this opinion as "omnino verum" in both contentious and criminal causes, whether for absolution or condemnation. Roberti [21] follows the same, declaring that the opinion of St. Thomas, which appears to be "verior et tutior," is now confirmed by the absolute disposition of Canon 1869, § 2.

[15] Bouix, *op. cit.*, I, p. 142; Wernz-Vidal, *op. cit.*, n. 591.
[16] *Theologia Moralis,* IV, n. 208.
[17] Wernz-Vidal, *op. cit.*, n. 591.
[18] *Op. cit.*, I, t. 32, n. 46.
[19] *Op. cit.*, I, t. 32, nn. 9, 10.
[20] *Op. cit.*, n. 622.
[21] *Op. cit.*, n. 448, note 3.

§ 2. *Matrimonial Causes*

If the third opinion (that of Lessius) is to be admitted, it would apply to causes *de statu personarum* because they are of greater consequence than grave criminal causes. These causes never become *res iudicata,*[22] and they are usually enumerated as: causes concerning matrimony, sacred orders and religious profession.[23] Important factors, which do not apply to other causes enter into these. In passing sentence the dominant element of the sentence is the objective truth which supersedes the other element, the legal command.[24] The explanation of the exception of these causes from becoming *res iudicata* is that canon law has always recognized that it cannot alter the truth of a matter of divine law by a human decision. Thus it is a notable fact that in matrimonial causes the sentence has never had any prescriptive effect on the case; and at any epoch in ecclesiastical jurisdiction, a sentence for either the existence or non-existence of marriage could be reversed when it was proved that the judge was deceived, or that there was error. The principle was followed that in spiritual things only the truth can prevail.[25] There is involved the question of sin; and it cannot be admitted that the sentence has power to keep people in the state of mortal sin. A sentence which fosters sin lacks stability, as Sanchez [26] points out:

> Quare sententia per errorem decidens illud esse validum, vel hoc dissolvendum, nulla ratione assumere potest vires rei iudicatae, sive quod bis confirmata sit, sive quod ab ea non appellans censeatur consentire. Quia sententia illa, transiens in rem iudicatam, foveret peccatum, separando veros coniuges, vel uniendo eos qui tales esse nequeunt. At nullum vinculum, quantumcumque multiplicatum, potest firmare actum, ex quo peccatum consurgit.

[22] Canon 1903.

[23] Vermeersch-Creusen, *op. cit.,* III, n. 245; Noval, *op. cit.*, n. 675; Dec. XIX, n. 4—*S. R. Rotae Decisiones seu Sententiae* (1922).

[24] *Cf.* Art. 1, Origin and Use of Term, Chapter I.

[25] Esmein, *Le Mariage en Droit Canonique,* p. 462, Hostiensis, *Summa Aurea,* p. 385.

[26] *De Sancto Matrimonii Sacramento Disputationum,* VII, d. C, n. 1; *Cf.* Gasparri, *De Matrimonio,* n. 1284; Dec. XIX, n. 4—*S. R. Rotae Decisiones seu Sententiae* (1922).

Panormitanus [27] affirms the same principle. No sentence given *in foro externo* could justify a person in prolonging a relation which he knew was no true marriage, and rather than be a party to it, he should suffer excommunication and die thus.[28] St. Alphonsus [29] considers it intrinsically evil for a judge to act against his private knowledge and force a false conjugal union.

§ 3. *Conclusion*

The discussion about the use of private knowledge is for the most part purely speculative. In practice, private knowledge has no part in the judicial acts;[30] and should such a conflict arise, the difficulty can be obviated. Excepting in minor contentious causes, the judge would be obliged to use every means to establish his private knowledge in a judicial way. This could be effected by several means. The judge could protract the hearing, examine more closely the witnesses and the testimony and ask pertinent questions to bring out the truth. Or again, he could declare himself incompetent, and at the hearing before another judge, he could testify of his personal knowledge on the matter.[31] Hence, the opinion of St. Thomas stands vindicated as the practical solution in accordance with the Code; and the judge is always obliged as a public official to form his judgment *ex actis et probatis*.

Art. 4. Proofs, the Motives of Certitude

§ 1. *Notions*

Closely allied to moral certitude is proof since the latter is to the former, as cause is to effect. They are perforce of the same order; and therefore, for moral certitude is required such proof as will exclude any prudent doubt of error. Proof may be defined as "the

[27] *Commentaria in quinque Libros Decretalium,* V, p. 87, on c. 10, n. 6, X, *de sent. et re iud.*, II, 27.

[28] C. 44, X, *de sent. excommunicationis,* V, 39; Joyce, *Christian Marriage,* p. 109.

[29] *Theologia Moralis,* IV, n. 208.

[30] *Glossa,* c. 1, *de sent. et re iud.*, II, 14 in VI°.

[31] Santi, *Praelectiones Iuris Canonici,* I, t. 32, n. 13.

solution of a doubt or controversy by legitimate arguments propounded before the judge."[32] Thus, from it flows the moral persuasion which moves the judge to a decision. The general norm for determining the effectiveness or valuation of proof is the deep personal conscientious conviction of the judge, with the exception that in cases where the Code expressly determines the value of certain proofs, the norm is the value stated in the law.[33] In practice it is found that as an aid to the judge, Canon law has defined legal proofs and their effectiveness quite comprehensively.

Proofs may be *direct* or *indirect*. The direct proof immediately appertains to the controverted fact. Indirect proofs pertain to another fact from which a deduction throws light on the main fact to be established. All indirect proofs are presumptions. Direct proofs are either *simplices,* which are propounded in the trial, *e. g.*, confession, personal testimony, oaths, expert testimony, judicial interrogation; or *praeconstitutae,* which are existent before the trial, *e. g.*, documents.[34]

Another classification is full proof (*plena*) and partial proof (*semi-plena*). Some authors before the Code recognized only full proof, and anything that fell short of it was no proof.[35] Others graduated proofs into several classes, viz., *plena, semi-plena, plus quam semi-plena, et minus quam semi-plena.*[36] Full proof is that which completely persuades the judge of the truth of the controverted issue so that nothing further is needed to pass sentence or settle the issue. Partial proof is that which very probably reveals the truth, but not certainly.[37] When a proof is produced which is not expressly defined in the Code, it is for the judge to evaluate that proof, *i. e.*, whether it be full, partial, or no proof.[38] Considering all facts and circumstances, the judge is to be guided by the light of his reason and

[32] Lega, *op. cit.*, I, n. 434.

[33] C. 1869, § 3; *cf.* c. 6, X, *de renunciatione,* I, 9; c. 27, X, *de testibus et attestationibus,* II, 20.

[34] Roberti, *op. cit.*, n. 324.

[35] Bouix, *op. cit.*, I, p. 303.

[36] Schmalzgrueber, *op. cit.*, II, t. 19, n. 14.

[37] Bouix, *op. cit.*, I, p. 303.

[38] Canon 1869, § 3.

is to arrive at his own conscientious estimation.[39] Where the law expressly determines the effectiveness of certain proofs, the judge is to valuate them according to the evident provisions therein stated.[40]

§ 2. *Legal Proofs*

The legal proofs determined by the Code are either *plena* or *semi-plena*. The *plena* or full proofs are: confession in a private affair (Canon 1751), presumptive confession from refusal to give handwriting (Canon 1800, § 4), depositions of two absolutely trustworthy witnesses (Canon 1791, § 2), depositions of one qualified witness given *ex officio* (Canon 1791, § 1), public documents (Canon 1816), presumptions *iuris et de iure* (Canon 1826), decisive oaths (Canon 1836, § 2), failure to make retorted decisive oath (Canon 1836, § 4), notorious facts (Canon 1747, § 1). The Code attributes the force of partial proof (*semi-plena*) to the following: supplementary oath (Canon 1829), presumptions of law (Canon 1827), deposition of one witness (Canon 1791, § 1), testimony of the *septimae manus* (Canon 1975, § 2). The Code leaves to the estimation of the judge the following: extra-judicial confession (Canon 1753), refusal to produce documents (Canon 1824, § 2), refusal to make supplementary oath (Canon 1831, § 2) or decisive oath (Canon 1836, § 3), private documents (Canon 1817).[41]

§ 3. *General Principles for Valuation of Proofs*

Many useful general principles for determining the force of proofs are to be found in Canon law and in the recommendations of commentators. A few of the more important will be enumerated:

(*a*) Status of witnesses. Canon law recognizes the variable effectiveness of qualitative and quantitative proof, and it gives the greater force to qualitative proof.[42] Such qualities in witnesses as

[39] Noval, *op. cit.*, n. 623.

[40] Roberti, *op. cit.*, n. 448; Noval, *op. cit.*, n. 623.

[41] Roberti, *op. cit.*, n. 328; *cf.* Noval, *op. cit.*, n. 623.

[42] Canon 1730; c. 32, X, *de testibus et attestationibus*, II, 20.

honesty, state in life, official position, reliability, lend force to testimony.[43] When witnesses contradict one another, credence is to be given accordingly as persons are trustworthy and better qualified, and as their evidence is more likely to be true.[44]

(*b*) Personal knowledge. Direct knowledge has more weight than indirect. Rumors and reports related by witnesses lack the force of personal knowledge. Eye-witnesses and auditors are the most effective witnesses;[45] but this does not exclude other kinds of witnesses.[46] Where the proofs are objectively equal, that of an eye-witness is of greater force than that of another mode of knowledge.[47]

(*c*) Consistency and coherence. These are important qualities in testimony, and where they are found, they go a great way to confirm the reliability and truth of the evidence and to establish the required certitude in the mind of the judge.[48] Usually reliability is to be given according to the agreement of the greater numbers, especially when collusion is out of the question; but numbers yield to fewer and better qualified witnesses.[49]

(*d*) Contradictory proofs. Two equal contradictory proofs nullify each other.[50] Attempt should be made to reconcile discrepancies when they arise.[51] If this is impossible, "maiorem probationem praeferendam esse minori." [52] When the contradiction arises between a full proof and a partial proof, the full proof destroys the partial proof.[53]

(*e*) Partial proofs. In civil causes, two partial proofs with indications and presumptions all tending to verify the same fact may be accepted as full proof. In criminal causes, inferences, presumptions

[43] Canon 1789, § 1. "Condicio, sexus, aetas, discretio, fama et fortuna, fides: in testibus ista requires"—*glossa*, c. 2, X, *de testibus et attestationibus*, II, 20.

[44] C. 32, X, *de testibus et attestationibus*, II, 20.

[45] Canon 1789, § 2.

[46] Noval, *op. cit.*, n. 510.

[47] Heiner, *De Processu Criminali Ecclesiastico*, p. 115.

[48] *Cf.* Canon 1789, § 3.

[49] C. 32, X, *de testibus et attestationibus*, II, 20; *cf.* Canon 1789, § 4.

[50] C. ult. X, *de sent. et re iud.*, II, 27.

[51] C. 13, X, *de restitutione spol.*, II, 13.

[52] C. 3, X, *de causa possess.*, II, 12.

[53] C. 9, X, *de probationibus*, II, 19.

and conjectures may serve as aids to effect full proof when with other evidences they give moral certainty.[54]

(*f*) Precedent. To follow the practice of the Rota in its published decisions,[55] may often be helpful in arriving at the proper estimation of certain proofs. The practice of the Rota in a particular case bears with it no legal authorization of itself, but it may often offer a norm of procedure when an explicit provision of law is lacking.[56] Hence where an intrinsic analogy may be found in a decision of the Rota on some specific kind of proof, then the estimation accepted in the Rota would be reliable. If the cause with all its proof is intrinsically analogous with that settled in a decision of the Rota, then there would be found a reasonable precedent for a similar decision in the diocesan tribunal.[57]

Art. 5. Rules for Doubtful Cases

§ 1. *General Principle*

Canon 1869, § 4, is in accord with and flows from the general principles laid down in the Code, viz., "onus probandi incumbit ei qui asserit,"[58] "actore non probante reus absolvitur."[59] Excepting favorable causes, *i. e.*, matrimony, privilege of faith and liberty, the solution of doubtful cases due to the lack of moral certitude in the mind of the judge is to be in favor of the defendant. After thorough investigation in the trial, certitude may be wanting because of deficiency of the necessary proof; which deficiency arises when no legal proof (*probatio plena ex lege*) is established and the evidence produced has no sufficient objective and subjective force to persuade the judge. An absolutory sentence is then to be pronounced and the defendant freed.[60]

[54] Heiner, *op. cit.*, pp. 34, 35, 115.

[55] *S. R. Rotae Decisiones seu Sententiae.*

[56] *Cf.* Canons 17, § 3, 20; Michiels, *Normae Generales*, I, pp. 397, 398.

[57] *Cf.* Michiels, *op. cit.*, I, pp. 475, 476; S. d'Angelo, *Saggi su Questioni Giuridiche*, pp. 83, 84.

[58] Canon 1748, § 1.

[59] Canon 1748, § 2.

[60] Noval, *op. cit.*, n. 624.

§ 2. *Effects of an Absolutory Sentence*

Canonists do not agree as to whether the effects of the absolutory sentence are *ab impetitione actoris* (definitely settling the merit of the issue), or *ab observatione iudicii* (temporarily closing the case *in instantia* and leaving the issue in suspense). Noval [61] and Roberti [62] hold that it is absolutory *ab impetitione actoris*. Muniz [63] and Vidal [64] take the opinion that in causes of private good it is absolutory *ab impetitione actoris;* but that in causes of crime, of *status personarum* and in those involving directly the public good, it is absolutory *ab observatione iudicii*. After considering all possible elements of a cause, the judge should definitely settle the merit of the issue because otherwise the rights of the parties might remain forever uncertain and open to question. The law provides for causes of *status personarum,* and in all causes it allows proper recourse against the sentence. Hence the opinion of Noval and Roberti seems to be the more sound.

§ 3. *Favorable Causes*

Causes enjoying the favor of the law (*causae favorabiles*) are excepted from the general rule of favoring the defendant, so that in case of doubt the sentence must be given in their support. The favor of the law is usually based on a presumption of law which, unless the contrary is proved, determines the sentence.[65] The causes enjoying the favor of the law in the Code are:

(1) Matrimonial causes. Marriage when once contracted and having the *species matrimonii* is in possession and it is presumed to be validly contracted until the contrary is proven; hence the sentence must be in favor of validity whenever moral certainty of invalidity is lacking.[66]

[61] *Op. cit.*, n. 624.

[62] *Op. cit.*, n. 449.

[63] *Procedimientos Eclesiasticos,* III, n. 439.

[64] Wernz-Vidal, *op. cit.*, n. 589, note 19.

[65] Roberti, *op. cit.*, n. 450.

[66] Canon 1014; Gasparri, *op. cit.*, n. 18 ff.; Ayrinhac-Lydon, *Marriage Legislation in the New Code of Canon Law,* p. 7.

(2) Privilege of faith. Canon 1127: "In re dubia privilegium fidei gaudet favore iuris." The favor of law allowed in this canon is not merely of ecclesiastical law, but is based on divine law.[67] The privilege of faith in a broad sense favors that solution of a doubtful case which is most conducive to the acquisition, profession and extension of the true faith.[68] In a technical sense it is the favor of the law extended to a convert so that: either, doubtful previous marriage may be validated so long as there is not involved an impediment, from which the Holy See certainly cannot dispense; or, in case of doubt of the applicability of the Pauline Privilege, he may use it.[69] If the danger of attempting the dissolution of matrimony *ratum et consummatum* is involved, *e. g.*, doubtful baptism of both parties with subsequent cohabitation, the privilege is not applicable. It has been the constant policy of the Holy See not to attempt the dissolution of a *possibly* indissoluble marriage bond.[70] In applying the privilege of faith the marriage of the convert is validated either by force of the Pauline Privilege or by the force of the implicit indult of the Holy See.[71] Competency to handle causes referring to the Pauline Privilege is restricted to the Holy See.[72]

(3) Liberty. Liberty is always to be vindicated in regard to penalties, and generally in regard to moral matters. No penalty is to be inflicted until it is proven that the crime was certainly committed, and that prosecution is not barred by legitimate prescription.[73]

In the old law many other favorable causes were enumerated, viz., causes referring to wills, testaments, minors, aliment of widows and orphans, pious causes, etc. Today these matters are usually brought up in civil courts; but if they should be presented in ecclesiastical

[67] *Periodica,* X (1922), (25)-(26).

[68] *Cf. NRT,* LII (1925), 227 ff.

[69] *Cf.* Payen, *De Matrimonio,* II, n. 2415 (bis); *Ius Pont.,* XII (1932), 114 ff.; *ETL,* III (1926), 328; Gregory, *The Pauline Privilege,* p. 110 ff.

[70] *ETL,* I (1924), 174 ff.; Vromant, *Ius Missionariorum,* V, n. 294; Payen, *op. cit.,* II, n. 2415 (bis); *NRT,* LII (1925), 217 ff.

[71] Wernz, *Ius Decretalium,* IV, n. 702, note 66; *Ius Pont.,* XII (1932), p. 114.

[72] Canon 1962.

[73] Canon 2233, § 1.

courts, it seems advisable that the statutes and practice of the civil law should be observed. The same holds true for the treatment of incidental questions about civil effects in matrimonial causes.[74] The civil law, as a rule, makes ample provision for the protection of rights in all these matters.

§ 4. *Possessory Causes*

In causes referring to retention of possession, the doubt is to be solved by giving, as the case may be, joint possession of the thing to the contending parties or equal right in it.[75]

§ 5. *Variation in Degree of Certitude*

It is obvious that the force of evidence required for different causes may vary according to the gravity of the nature of the cause treated. To pass sentence upholding nullity in a matrimonial cause, there would be required such a preponderance of evidence as would exclude any reasonable doubt in the mind of the judge. The same holds true in regard to passing a condemnatory sentence in a criminal trial. However, in regard to contentious causes, especially those of little moment, it seems that simply a preponderance of evidence should suffice to determine the decision of the judge. Matters of great moment would require certitude from clear and satisfactory evidence. This procedure is supported by the condemnation by Innocent XI of the proposition that a judge could decide a contentious cause on arguments which were less probable; and thereby, the contradictory opinion admitting more probable proofs as a basis for decision is upheld.[76] Our civil courts are in accord with this procedure.

[74] Roberti, *op. cit.*, n. 450; *cf.* Canons 1513, 1529, 1961.

[75] Canon 1697, § 2.

[76] Denziger, n. 1152; *cf.* Bouix, *op. cit.*, II, p. 227; Schmalzgrueber, *op. cit.*, II, t. 27, n. 28.

CHAPTER VI

REGULATIONS ON THE DELIBERATIONS OF THE JUDGES (CANONS 1870-1872)

ART. 1. THE TRIBUNAL OF ONE JUDGE

Canon 1870. Sententia ferri a iudice debet, expleta causae disceptatione; et si causa sit implicatior et contentionum vel documentorum mole difficilior, interponi potest congruum temporis intervallum.

Canon 1872. Si unicus sit iudex, ipsius tantum est sententiam exarare; in tribunali vero collegiali servetur prescriptum Can. 1584.

The judge should pass sentence as quickly as possible after the close of the final pleading in which the advocates of the parties present their final defenses and the promoter of justice or defender of the bond, if participating, presents his final brief and declares that he is satisfied to rest the case. No definite time is specified in the canons, but obviously from the nature of the matter, it should be expedited to the greatest extent compatible with the due observance of the requirements of law and justice. At times in contentious causes the parties may forego the presentation of their final defense, or they may neglect to prepare it; then the judge, if he has sufficient knowledge of the case, may immediately pronounce sentence.[1] In complicated and difficult causes the judge may allow himself a reasonable interval of time to study the cause and to inspect and to weigh the evidence carefully. Should the judge prove himself negligent or delay too much unnecessarily in giving the sentence, recourse may be had to the Ordinary. The judge may have two councillors (*assessores*), who are to be chosen from among the synodal judges, to assist him in a purely consultive capacity.[2] The councillors have

[1] Canon 1867.

[2] Canon 1575.

no deliberative vote; it is for the judge alone to decide the issue, and it is his duty to draw up the sentence, which should be in Latin.[3]

ART. 2. DELIBERATION OF THE COLLEGIATE TRIBUNAL

Canon 1871, § 1. In tribunali collegiali, qua die et hora iudices ad deliberandum conveniant, collegii, praeses constituat; et nisi peculiaris causa aliud suadeat, in ipsa tribunalis sede conventus habeatur.

§ 2. Assignata conventui die, singuli iudices scriptas afferent conclusiones suas in merito causae, et rationes tam in facto quam in iure, quibus ad conclusionem suam venerint: quae conclusiones actis causae adiungantur, secreto servandae.

§ 3. Prolatis ex ordine, secundum praecedentiam, ita tamen ut semper a causae ponente seu relatore initium fiat, singulorum conclusionibus, habeatur moderata discussio sub tribunalis praesidis ductu, praesertim ut constabiliatur quid statuendum sit in parte dispositiva sententiae.

§ 4. In discussione autem fas unicuique est a pristina sua conclusione recedere.

§ 5. Quod si iudices in prima discussione ad hanc sententiam devenire aut nolint aut nequeant, differri poterit decisio ad novum conventum; qui tamen ultra hebdomadam comperendinari non debet.

Canon 1584. Tribunalis collegialis praeses debet unum de iudicibus collegii ponentem seu relatorem designare qui in coetu iudicium de causa referat et sententias in scriptis redigat; et ipsi idem praeses potest alium ex iusta causa substituere.

§ 1. *Time and Place of Deliberation*

The same principle of judicious celerity in passing sentence holds for the collegiate tribunal as for the tribunal of one judge. After the close of the final pleading, with the defender of the bond or promoter of justice, if either participate, satisfied to conclude the cause,

[3] Canon 1642, § 2; Heiner, *op. cit.*, p. 117.

a copy of the defences is given to each judge in order that he may thoroughly study the cause.[4] The *relator* (or *ponens*) may be appointed by the *officialis* or presiding judge at this time, if this has not already been done. Noval[5] prudently recommends that the *relator* be appointed at the beginning of the trial because it is highly expedient that he take a special interest throughout the trial in observing the interrogation, in noting the principal proofs, in observing the progress of the cause, etc. The presiding judge, with due consideration for the complicated nature of the evidence and for the gravity and difficulty of the question to be solved, sets the day and the hour for the meeting of the judges to deliberate on the sentence. This interval between the conclusion of the pleading and the deliberation of the judges should be such as to give ample opportunity for the judges to study thoroughly the facts and merits of the cause and the points of law involved. Unwarranted and unreasonable delays should be avoided. If such delays should occur, it seems proper that the interested parties should file protest with the tribunal; and if this proved unavailing, then protest should be made to the Ordinary. The usual place for the meeting is where the court sessions are held. A matter of convenience would justify it being held elsewhere, provided the efficiency of the tribunal would not be impaired. Only the judges of the cause under consideration are to be present; the parties, the promoter of justice or the defender of the bond, and even the notary have no right to be present, and should be excluded.[6] The reason for this exclusion of the other court officials is that the judges may have complete freedom in expressing their opinions and discussing the cause, the solution of which is exclusively their concern.

§ 2. *Procedure at the Meeting of Judges*

In the interval before the appointed day of the meeting, each judge, after complete study of the cause, should draw up in writing his personal conclusion with the statement of the reasons of law and fact upon which it is based. As the meeting opens the *relator* gives a brief review of the cause. In the brief review he points out

[4] Canon 1863, § 1.

[5] *Op. cit.*, n. 137.

[6] Roberti, *op. cit.*, n. 455; Muniz, *op. cit.*, n. 441; *Regulae servandae in iudiciis apud S. R. Rotae Tribunal*, § 177, n. 1.

the purpose and nature of the petition, the admissions and denials of the defendant, the concessions made by the parties, the proofs adduced and their value, the stand taken and the defense made by the contestants, what incidental questions arose and their solution, what questions remain to be settled and reasons for such, and any defects in procedure which may exist.[7] It often may be advisable for the *relator* to review the same points with the other judges at earlier periods of the trial.[8] When the *relator* concludes the outline of the cause, the meeting proceeds with the presentation and reading of the written conclusions of each judge. First the *relator* reads his conclusion which contains his vote or opinion with the reasons of fact and law. Then the presiding judge reads his, and the other judges follow suit according to their precedence. The *relator* gives his conclusion first because this office should be filled by the judge who is most proficient in Canon law.

These provisions of the Code are drawn from those of the Roman tribunals:

> Primus sermonem instituit Ponens, qui legit votum, opportunis factis declarationibus, etiam super causae processu per acta apud se posita. Deinde ceteri Auditores, ex ordine, prosequuntur sua vota legere eaque declarare, si opus sit.[9]

Discussion is now in order under the direction of the presiding judge. The chief object of the discussion is to determine definitely the decisive part of the sentence, and also, if possible, to clear up any discrepancies; it may likewise be advisable practice to determine the narrative part, *i. e.*, the motives to be appended by the *relator*. During the discussion any judge may change any part or the whole of his original conclusion; which change does not necessitate the separate committing to writing of the fact in a new conclusion, as the new vote with its reasons of law and fact are to be appended to the original conclusion.[10] The *Rules* of the Rota clearly indicate the procedure:

[7] Muniz, *op. cit.*, n. 441; Wernz-Vidal, *op. cit.*, n. 594.

[8] Noval, *op. cit.*, n. 137.

[9] *Regulae servandae in iudiciis apud S. R. Rotae Tribunal*, § 178, n. 1; *cf. Lex propria S. R. Rotae et Signaturae Ap.*, C. 31, §§ 1, 2.

[10] Wernz-Vidal, *op. cit.*, n. 594; Roberti, *op. cit.*, n. 455; Lyons, *op. cit.*, p. 68.

> Si decisiones inter se discrepent, et nascatur discussio, fas est Auditoribus a suo voto partim vel ex integro recedere; ast mutationes inductae et rationes significari breviter debent in voto scripto sub formula "*Accedo voto Domini . . . et ob rationes in eodem voto expressas,* vel *ob . . .*" [11]

After the discussion a new vote is to be taken, if any of the original conclusions were changed. The outcome gives the final disposition of the cause and it forms the dispositive part of the sentence, which is to be drawn up by the *relator.* If there is lacking clear uniformity and agreement in the motives stated in the conclusions of the judges, it seems advisable that the judges should at least indicate what motives are to be incorporated in the narrative part of the sentence by the *relator.*

§ 3. *Second and Succeeding Meetings*

It is not imperative that the judges decide the cause at the first meeting for deliberation. If, therefore, at the first meeting, the judges either cannot reach a decision or wish to allow more time for further private or collective deliberation, they may call one or two meetings so long as they do not delay beyond a week from the first meeting.[12] The limit of one week is not imposed peremptorily, and therefore, for grave reasons the time may be lengthened.[13] However, except under very unusual or impossible circumstances, it seems that one week should be the ultimate limit of delay. The provisions of the Code (Canon 1871, § 5) are similar to those stated in the *Rules* of the Rota:

> Quoties in prima discussione haberi non potest maior pars votorum necessaria causae decisioni, differtur iudicium turno qui proxime habebitur per rescriptum "*Resolutio dabitur in proximo Auditorum conventu,*" aut simpliciter, "*Dabitur in proximo.*"
>
> Decreta dilatione ad *proximum* turni conventum, hunc protrahere non licet ultra hebdomadam, nisi forte vacationes tribunalis intercedant (Canon 31, § 4, Lex propria).[14]

[11] *Regulae servandae in iudiciis apud S. R. Rotae Tribunal,* § 178, n. 2.

[12] Noval, *op. cit.,* n. 626.

[13] Roberti, *op. cit.,* n. 455.

[14] *Regulae servandae in iudiciis apud S. R. Rotae Tribunal,* § 178, nn. 3, 4.

§ 4. *Vote Necessary for Decision*

For the collegiate tribunal to reach a decision in regard to the sentence, there is required a majority of votes.[15] This majority must be absolute.[16] A relative majority will not suffice. The collegiate tribunal is not to be considered as a moral person in the strict sense, *i. e.*, as defined by the Code,[17] and any analogy drawn from the rules in voting by moral persons cannot be admitted as applicable to the collegiate tribunal.[18] Hence, such prescriptions, as the transmission of rights to surviving members of collegiate moral persons,[19] and the validity of a relative majority in the third voting,[20] do not apply to judicial procedure.

To arrive at an absolute majority should not, in practice, offer any particular difficulty. It may be in complicated causes that one or more of the judges will not, because of doubts, give a decisive vote. Thus, the tribunal may be deadlocked for one or several deliberative meetings in an effort to clear points of law and to appraise the evidence. However, unless extraneous factors arise, the week allowed for these deliberations should be ample, and a decision should be given. If a judge is of doubtful mind after the thorough investigation and mature deliberation, then he should cast his vote in accord with the principles enunciated in Canon 1869, § 4.

§ 5. *Ways of Relieving a Deadlocked Tribunal*

Some helpful norms for relieving a deadlocked tribunal may be drawn from the provisions of procedure of the Rota:

> Si in secundo quoque Auditorum conventu, haberi non possit pars maior votorum necessaria ad decisionem, quum singuli Auditores dent dubiis propositis diversas respon-

[15] Canon 1577, § 1.

[16] *Regulae servandae in iudiciis apud S. R. Rotae Tribunal,* § 176; *Lex Propria S. R. Rotae et Signaturae Ap.*, C. 31, § 3.

[17] Canon 100.

[18] *Cf.* Roberti, *op. cit.*, n. 451; Noval, *op. cit.*, n. 126; Wernz-Vidal, *op. cit.*, n. 595.

[19] Canon 102, § 2.

[20] Canon 101, § 1, n. 1.

> siones; perpendatur utrum expediat, vel alia documenta aut probationes exquirere in declarationem cuiusdam facti controversi, vel partes invitare ad magis specificam dubiorum concordationem; nisi apportunius sit, quaestionis solutionem differre per rescriptum: *Dilata*, aut *Reproponatur*, aut *Non constare*, aut *Non satis constare*. Quod si nullum ex his remediis ad optatum exitum conducere valeat, Ponens Domino Decano significabit statum quaestionis, ut ad normam quoque can. 11 (Lex propria) aliter provideatur.[21] (Canon 11 provides that a decision may be given *videntibus omnibus*.)[22]

The Ordinary may add some other judges to the deadlocked tribunal as Canon 1576, § 2, allows. Authors [23] remark that this is of no great practical value, because it is limited in its application, and then when applied, it may only infrequently solve the difficulty. The Ordinary may submit a cause to at most five judges,[24] and therefore the only practical case consists of adding two judges to a collegiate tribunal of three judges; which procedure may or may not be effective. Muniz [25] takes the view that, if after seven days no decision is reached, the Ordinary appoint a new collegiate group of judges to decide the cause. In regard to adding judges or appointing new judges to relieve a deadlocked tribunal, Roberti [26] states that while it is licit procedure it can scarcely be said to be juridic and is not always effective. It is his opinion that in every case the judges proper to the trial can legitimately pass sentence and should do so.

Inviting the parties to make a more specific agreement on the issues of the case may sometimes serve to clear up the points of disagreement among the judges. Also, the judges may re-open a cause to admit new proofs and documents. However, after the conclusion of the cause, new evidence is not to be admitted except in causes which do not become *res iudicata*, or unless documents were just

[21] *Regulae servandae in iudiciis apud S. R. Rotae Tribunal*, § 180.

[22] *Lex propria S. R. Rotae et Signaturae Ap.*, c. 11.

[23] Muniz, *op. cit.*, n. 442; Wernz-Vidal, *op. cit.*, n. 595, note 48.

[24] Canon 1576, § 2.

[25] Muniz, *op. cit.*, 442.

[26] *Op. cit.*, n. 444.

newly discovered or witnesses could not be previously introduced in the proper time because of a legitimate impediment.[27] The party against whom the evidence is directed is to be heard on the admission of the evidence and, if it is admitted, he is to be allowed sufficient time to consider the new proofs and to defend himself.[28] From these limitations it is to be noted that the judges, in order to clear up disagreements among themselves, are completely free only to open up causes which do not become *res iudicata*. Since matrimonial causes are of this class, the procedure may be helpful at times. However, precautions should be taken to have a thorough and complete investigation of all evidence when it is first being made. It becomes evident, then, that during the trial the *relator* should closely observe the taking of testimony, so as to bring to light any hidden facts which later may be pertinent in discerning the cause for judgment.

When judges agree substantially on an issue, but disagree on accidental limits to be imposed, a specific solution may be reached by a proportioned compromise. For instance, it is agreed that the defendant is to be condemned to pay damages. One judge holds for assessing $100; another for $200; the third for $300. The proportionately compromised amount of damages would be $200, which amount should be imposed.[29]

An unusual case may arise when the tribunal is composed of an even number of judges, and an even vote ensues. This might occur in case of suspicion being raised against one of the delegated judges,[30] and two judges uphold the exception with the two others opposed. The solution may be given on the principle "actore non probante, reus absolvitur," and the exception is over-ruled..[31]

§ 6. *Presentation of Question*

In voting upon the incidental or final causes presented to the tribunal, it is necessary that a separate vote be made on each specific question. Hence, if several causes were presented to sustain the peti-

[27] *Cf.* Canon 1861, § 1.
[28] *Cf.* Canon 1861, § 2.
[29] *Cf.* Roberti, *op. cit.*, n. 453.
[30] Canon 1614, § 1.
[31] *Cf.* Roberti, *op. cit.*, n. 454.

tion, each cause is to be separately proposed to the judges for a vote.[82]

The case might arise when a petition for the declaration of nullity of marriage is based on two causes: *ex capite impotentiae et ex capite vis et metus.* If the formula proposed was "An constat de nullitate matrimonii in casu," the vote might eventuate thus: (1-to-1-to-1)—one vote might be for validity, one for nullity *ex capite impotentiae,* and the third for nullity *ex capite vis et metus.* Hence there would appear a fictitious majority for nullity. If the formula was proposed under each title separately, the voting in each cause would be two for validity, and one for nullity. Only in the latter presentation is there to be had a valid sentence; the former could yield no sentence at all as the foundation of the sentence is lacking.[83]

When there is only one cause proposed as the basis of the petition, then the formula "An constat de nullitate matrimonii in casu" is specific and suffices. Nevertheless, it may be prudent procedure to add the title—"ex capite . . . "[84]

When it happens that in the same process there are several decisions to be made, *e. g.*, the principal action, a counter-action, the intervention of a third party, etc., precaution should be taken to propose each question separately. From the particular decisions, the judges can readily arrive at the final conclusive solution.[85] This method will tend to obviate difficulties which may arise from lack of definitiveness and precision in a sentence.

Art. 3. Secrecy

§ 1. *Provisions of Secrecy for the Whole Process*

Before taking up the provisions of secrecy governing the deliberations and the private conclusions of the collegiate judges, it is pertinent to mention the privisions of secrecy for the process in general. Just protection of the rights of individuals participating in ecclesiasti-

[82] Roberti, *op. cit.*, n. 452; Cappello, *De Sacramentis,* III, n. 887; *Periodica,* XX (1931), 20 ff.

[83] Roberti, *op. cit.*, n. 452; Cappello, *op. cit.*, III, n. 887.

[84] Cappello, *op. cit.*, n. 887; *Periodica,* XX (1931), 20 ff.

[85] Roberti, *op. cit.*, n. 452.

cal trials is amply provided for them by Canon law. In criminal causes, the judges and all those assisting the tribunal are obliged *ex officio* to observe secrecy about all that transpires in or is connected with the trial.[36] When the sentence is published, unless a special precept is given to the contrary, the officials of the court are not obliged to secrecy in those matters, which, by the sentence itself, become juridically public; the obligation still binds in regard to other matters.[37] In contentious causes, whenever the revelation of any of the acts of the trial might be injurious to the parties, the court officials are bound *ex officio* to secrecy.[38] In all trials, whenever the nature of the cause or of the evidence is such that the revelation of any of the preceedings may occasion injury to the reputation of others, or occasion discord, scandal or any other similar consequence, then the judge can bind the parties and their advocates, the witnesses, experts, etc., to observe secrecy by oath.[39] Violations of the *secretum officii* are punishable according to the prescriptions of the Code;[40] nor is there precluded the institution of action for damages by the injured parties.

§ 2. *The Provisions of Secrecy in Regard to the Discussions and Conclusions of the Judges*

Provisions for secrecy to govern the meeting of the collegiate judges for deliberation are laid down in Canon 1623, § 2:

> Tenentur [iudices et tribunalis adiutores] etiam semper ad inviolabile secretum servandum de discussione quae in tribunali collegiali ante ferendam sententiam habetur, tum etiam de variis suffragiis et opinionibus ibidem prolatis.

Provision to preserve the written private conclusions of the judges in secrecy is made in Canon 1871, § 2: " . . . quae conclusiones actis causae adiungantur, secreto servandae." In the prescription on the procedure of the Rota, point is made that the conclusions are to be kept in the secret archives:

[36] *Cf.* Canon 1623, § 1.
[37] Wernz-Vidal, *op. cit.*, n. 155.
[38] Canon 1623, § 1.
[39] Canon 1623, § 3.
[40] Canon 1625, § 2.

> Vota scripta dabuntur Ponenti aut Auditori cui sententiam exarare demandatum est. Publicata sententia, ista vota tradentur Domino Decano, a quo asservanda sunt in archivio secreto decanali (canon 31, § 2, Lex propria).[41]

In applying the provisions of the Code in practice, it is found that the exact extent to which they are to be observed is not always unquestionably evident for every contingency. Particularly do canonists offer divergent interpretations in regard to disclosing the private conclusions of the judges of a lower court to the court of appeal. Obviously the Code intends uniform procedure in preserving the precribed secrecy, and therefore, a definite limitation is to be sought in that interpretation, which will recommend itself as preferable to others from its concordance with the stated prescriptions of law and with the indications flowing from the very nature of the matters concerned.

That the Code should have the foregoing prescriptions of secrecy is postulated by prudence and justice. The public knowledge of the intimate discussions of the judges and of their dissenting votes would tend to impair the stability of the sentence in the minds of all interested parties. Confidence in a majority decision (2-to-1, 3-to-2) would be diminished with the result that, in the event of an unfavorable decision, the parties would be reluctant to submit to it. That such reaction would be inevitable, is evinced by the doubts and questions raised against the all too frequent 5-to-4 decisions of the United States Supreme Court. Hence in practice, the secrecy enshrouding the private deliberations of the judges removes the danger of personal insinuations being directed against the judges, and it fosters reverence and obedience to the decision pronounced by the court. Moreover, the ends of justice are more effectively served, in that it affords the judges complete and unrestrained freedom to discuss and vote on a cause from its purely objective merits without the pressure of even sub-conscious restraint, which might arise from possible outside influences such as public opinion, local authority, or superior tribunals. For these reasons secrecy becomes imperative, and what transpires at the private meeting of the judges is not to be made known outside.

[41] *Regulae servandae in iudiciis apud S. R. Rotae Tribunal,* § 178, n. 5.

A minority vote is not recorded in the final decision drawn up by the *relator*. A judge giving a minority vote is obliged to appear to be in accord with the majority decision. The *secretum officii* binds the judges perpetually and inviolably,[42] and the same holds for the other officials of the court, should they perchance be permitted to be present at the deliberations.[43]

In the discussion of these provisions of secrecy covering the ecclesiastical process, it must be kept in mind that they apply to all causes; and therefore, a sound appraisal of their force is to be had not merely in the light of the less consequential contentious causes, but rather of the more momentous ones, such as grave criminal trials.

§ 3. *Admission of Other Court Officials to the Deliberations*

While all of the assisting court officials, even the notary, are excluded from the deliberations of the collegiate judges,[44] there does not seem to be established such an absolute exclusion that they are not to be admitted under any conditions. The text of Canon 1623 allows this interpretation. In paragraph one it is prescribed, that the judges and the assisting court officials are bound to observe the *secretum officii;* then in paragraph two it is prescribed that they are to observe the secrecy binding in the deliberations. Thereby, it may be implied that other court officials besides the judges may at times be allowed to be present at the private deliberations.[45] However it seems that such practice should be looked upon as very unusual procedure, and ordinarily these officials should be excluded.

§ 4. *Inspection of the Private Conclusions of the Judges by the Defender of the Bond*

Then likewise, the question may be raised as to whether or not the *defensor vinculi* has any right to inspect the private written con-

[42] Blat, *De Processibus,* n. 92; Wernz-Vidal, *op. cit.,* n. 155; Connolly, *Appeals,* p. 97.

[43] Wernz-Vidal, *op. cit.,* n. 155.

[44] Canon 1871, § 2; *Regulae servandae in iudiciis apud S. R. Rotae Tribunal,* § 177, n. 1; Roberti, *op. cit.,* n. 455; Muniz, *op. cit.,* n. 441.

[45] Roberti, *Apollinaris,* I (1928), 189.

clusions of the judges. He has the right to inspect at anytime of the trial the acts of the cause,[46] and in Canon 1871, § 2, is the provision that the private conclusions are to be joined to the acts of the cause. But because of other factors, the conclusion does not follow. After the final defenses and before the tribunal can proceed to determine the sentence, the defender of the bond must dclare that he has no further inquiry or remarks to make.[47] With this declaration his function ceases, or at least is suspended, until the sentence is passed; then the duty to appeal may arise.[48] Then also, while the conclusions are to be joined to the acts of the cause, they are not integrated into the acts and do not become part of the *acta* properly so-called. The conclusions are to be enclosed in a separate sealed folio, and they are joined to the *acta* so that both may be preserved together in safe keeping in the archives. Hence, the defender of the bond has no right to demand that the conclusions be opened for his inspection. Nevertheless, since there seems to be indicated no absolute prohibition against allowing other court officials to inspect the conclusions, the defender of the bond may request to do so and the judges with good reason may grant the request so long as there is no special prohibition.[49] Such procedure may at times be helpful in attaining the supreme aim of all legislation for matrimonial causes—the objective truth. It may be an aid to the defender of the bond in fulfilling his office which should not be that of obstructing the tribunal with every possible triviality or technicality from declaring the nullity of marriage, but rather that of protecting the bond of marriage until its nullity is established with moral certitude by the elimination, after thorough investigation, of every reasonable possibility of error.

§ 5. *Inspection by the Appellate Court of the Private Conclusions of the Judges of the Lower Court*

In regard to the case of appeal, the question is raised as to what is to be done with the private conclusions of the judges.

[46] Canon 1969, § 1.

[47] Canon 1984, § 2.

[48] *Apollinaris*, I (1928), 188.

[49] *Apollinaris*, I (1928), 189.

Should the conclusions of the judges of the lower court be sent to the superior court with the *acta causae* which are required by canon 1890? The solution is to be found in the proper interpretation of the provision *secreto servandae*[50] and in its application to the requirements of an appeal.

Authors in defining the phrase *secreto servandae* give various limitations to it. Noval[51] explains the provision as meaning that the conclusions are never to be revealed to the parties or their advocates: "'Secreto': ita ut numquam communicentur partibus aut earum advocatis." Blat[52] holds the same limitation. This interpretation can hardly be reconciled with the more emphatic provisions laid down in Canon 1623, § 2, which make it apparent that something more is involved than simply keeping the conclusions secret from the parties and their advocates. This does not mean necessarily that Canon 1623, § 2, imposes an absolute secrecy, so that no one but the judges themselves are ever to see their conclusions; but it does indicate that the secrecy to be observed is of greater moment and more limited, than the statements of Noval and Blat imply. This matter has been discussed previously in this same chapter under the title, "The Provisions of Secrecy in Regard to the Discussions and Conclusions of Judges." Muniz[53] supports a stricter interpretation. Emphasizing the secrecy of the deliberations, he states that the conclusions are to be kept sealed in a folio placed in the secret archives, either joined to the *acta,* or separate from the *acta* with a notation in the *acta* indicating their location. He allows that the folio containing the conclusions is to be opened only by judicial decree. Roberti[54] leans toward a less strict interpretation, which is inferred from his comments on the opinion of Muniz: "Verum, quod sciamus, firmo manente secreto, tam graves cautelae in usu non sunt apud plura tribunalia."

As pertains to the case of appeal, Noval[55] would permit the con-

[50] Canon 1871, § 2.
[51] *Op. cit.,* n. 626.
[52] *Op. cit.,* n. 398.
[53] *Op. cit.,* III, n. 444.
[54] *Op. cit.,* n. 455, note 2.
[55] *Op. cit.,* n. 626.

clusions to be sent upon request to the court of appeal: "bene vero [communicentur], ni fallor, iudici superiori, eas, in casu appellationis, exquirenti." Muniz [56] takes the position that, in case of revising the sentence or of appeal, the sealed folio containing the conclusions may be inspected by decree of the judges. In appeal, request is made by the higher court to have the conclusions forwarded there from the lower court, and a decree of inspection is issued. He explains that the only reason for preserving the conclusions is that they may be available in case of appeal. This reason is not at all convincing. It would seem more likely that they are preserved for the protection of the judges. Should administrative action be taken against the judges on suspicion of irregularities or for incompetence in administration of office, then the private conclusions of a judge would stand as his safeguard against unjust incrimination. From the individual conclusions, a just and impartial examination would be assured each judge respectively. Thus, should the decisions of a lower court be frequently revised or reversed by the higher courts and doubts arise as to the ability of the judges of the lower court, a capable judge holding a minority decision is in a position to vindicate himself.

Connolly [57] after thorough discussion of opinions and points of law, concludes upon this question as follows:

> The conclusion, therefore, would *seem* to be that the judge *a quo* should remit the entire body of judicial acts, including the secret deliberations, opinions and discussions of the collegiate judges, to the tribunal of second instance.

The foregoing opinions, which so readily open the private conclusions of the judges of the lower court to the inspection of the superior courts, seem to depend to a great extent upon a broad interpretation of the provisions of the Code, made without due regard for the very nature of the matters involved. Perhaps the key to the solution of the question is to be found in the nature of an appeal. An appeal is not to be viewed merely as a remedy against an unjust sentence, but basically it is to be considered as a legal means of hav-

[56] *Op. cit.*, n. 444.

[57] *Op. cit.*, p. 98.

ing a new investigation of the controversy instituted. This is substantiated by Roberti, who states that:

> Appellatio hodie non amplius intelligitur ut querela contra iudicem inferiorem, sed potius tamquam petitio ut causa novo et pleniori examini subiiciatur. Unde iudex superior quamvis dicatur sententiam praecedentis instantiae confirmare aut reformare, revera in ius controversum directe pronuntiat.[58]

> Finis appellationis est duplex: primo ut corrigantur errores, secundo ut causa novo ac pleniori examini subiiciatur. At appellatio non debet intelligi tamquam recursus ob receptas iniurias contra iudicem inferiorem interpositus, sed tamquam medium a lege statutum ut rectius iustitiae administrationi consulatur.[59]

Therefore, to obtain a more perfect administration of justice, the appeal is directed towards the elimination of a possible erroneous correlation of the facts of a cause and the provisions of law. The application of the law by the sentence of the judges in the first instance may at times be faulty. That human judges may err, is axiomatic. The appeal proposes to eliminate, or at least reduce to a minimum, the human equation. This is particularly evident when a declaration of the nullity of marriage is pronounced in the sentence, because, in order to reduce, as far as practicable, the element of error to its most remote possibility, the Code[60] demands an appeal and a concurring sentence before the first sentence of nullity becomes operative. Here, as in all cases of appeal, the law is concerned with a new investigation of the objective merits of the cause.

Since the appeal is to be concerned with a re-examination of the objective merits of the cause, why bring in the subjective elements—the personal private conclusions of the judges of the lower court? There seems to be no sound juridic reason for such procedure. To admit the private conclusions to the inspection of

[58] *Op. cit.*, n. 58.
[59] *Op. cit.*, n. 467.
[60] Canons 1986, 1987.

the superior court, would be to invite the hazard of undue subjective influences. It is conceivable that the private conclusion of a judge, whose fame as a canonist is widely recognized, might be the dominant factor in determining the decision of the second instance. Then, there is the ever present possibility that it might encourage negligence in the thorough examination of the objective facts and in the studied application of the prescriptions of law, which are the essentials of all hearings. The statement that the private conclusions and deliberations might be helpful to the appellate judges, can hardly be construed as complimentary to their diligence and ability. Judges should be canonists of recognized merit and ability.[61]

However, it must be kept in mind that the great objective of all ecclesiastical judicial procedure—especially in those causes which do not become *res iudicata*—is to establish the objective truth. Conditions must be considered as they may exist. Therefore, if in some particular cause the private conclusions of the judges of the first instance may be deemed to be of assistance to the judges of the second instance in ascertaining the objective truth, the conclusions may be forwarded to the superior court upon request.

[61] Canons 1573, § 4; 1574, § 1.

CHAPTER VII

OBJECT AND FORM OF THE SENTENCE (CANONS 1873-1877)

ART. 1. OBJECT OF THE SENTENCE

§ 1. *Settlement of the Controversy*

Canon 1873, § 1. Sententia debet:

n. 1. Definire controversiam coram tribunali agitatam; hoc est reum absolvere vel condemnare quod attinet ad petitiones vel accusationes adversus eum prolatas, data singulis dubiis, seu controversiae articulis, congrua responsione;

n. 2. Determinare (saltem quatenus fas sit et materia patiatur), quid pars damnata dare, facere, praestare, aut pati debeat, aut a quo abstinere; itemque quo modo, loco vel tempore obligatio implenda sit; . . .

The object of the sentence is to settle, with due regard for the provisions of law and the rights of the parties, the controversy pleaded before the tribunal. Controversy arises when the rights and obligations of persons are disputed, or crime is charged, or the status of persons is questioned. A solution must be given because matters of such moment cannot be left in a state of uncertainty or doubt. The temporal and oftentimes spiritual welfare of individuals and society must be protected by the definite and positive solution through ecclesiastical procedure of a controversy. Hence, Canon 1873, § 1, n. 1, prescribes that the sentence must decide the controversy litigated in the trial; that is, it must condemn or absolve the defendant in regard to the matters petitioned or the accusations preferred against him, after pronouncing on each of the points of dispute or the doubts on which the controversy was based. In matrimonial causes there is no condemnation or absolution of the *pars conventa* properly so-called, and the issue made in the petition is solved by the sentence declaring that nullity of the marriage has or has not been established. There are two points to be noted in the provisions of Canon 1873, § 1, n. 1: the limitation placed on the controversy *coram tribunali agitatam;* and the response to be given to each of the doubts or points of dispute in the controversy.

The provision limiting the controversy to that litigated before the tribunal restricts the scope of the sentence so that it is only concerned with deciding that specific controversy, and therefore it is not within the province of the court to decide any other controversy, even though connected with the litigated controversy, unless it is legally interjected and argued in the trial.[1] Thereby the Code implies that the sentence must conform with the *libellus*. The limits of the controversy are determined in the *contestatio litis* (the joining of issues).[2] The *libellus* is definitely formulated and there is drawn up the formula of doubts or issues of dispute upon the solution of which the controversy depends. After the *contestatio litis*, changes in the *libellus* and new issues of dispute may be admitted by the judge only for a grave cause; they are made at the instance of the parties (*ad instantiam partis*), or at the instance of the defender of the bond or the promoter of justice.[3] In contentious causes the judge always proceeds *ad instantiam*, but in criminal and spiritual causes he may *ex officio* order changes in the issues, accusations or *libellus*, to which the sentence must then conform.[4] Incidental causes having a bearing on the principal cause may arise during a trial, and are to be decided before the final sentence.[5] The provision of Canon 1873, § 1, n. 1, in regard to the response or pronouncement to be given on each of the doubts or points of dispute does not seem to necessitate that a pronouncement be made on each specific point. A pronouncement on one point may be implicitly contained in the pronoucement on another point, or it may be so closely connected with the petition

[1] Noval, *De Processibus*, n. 628.

[2] Canons 1726 ff.

[3] Canons 1729, § 4; 1731, n. 1.

[4] Lega, *De Iudiciis Ecclesiasticiis*, I, n. 609; *cf.* Canon 1618.

[5] Canons 1837 ff.

that it is contained in the decision on the main question.[6] A pronouncement should be given on the other points of dispute. These judicial pronouncements are to be stated in the sentence before the main decision which contains the disposition of the controversy. If there are several integral points to the controversy, then a pronouncement is to be made on each specific point; these pronouncements then form the dispositive part of the sentence and give the solution of the controversy.

The response to each of the doubts or points of dispute does not necessarily include a response to the arguments proposed by the participants in the trial. Usually the responses to the doubts or points of dispute will implicitly contain a response to and an appraisal of the arguments. The judges in stating their motives for the decision will at least indirectly reply to the arguments. At times it may be necessary to give a direct reply to specific arguments expounded by the participants. This will depend upon the nature and the importance of the argument.

Canon 1873, § 1, n. 2, prescribes that the solution of the controversy must be precise and exhaustive. The trial is instituted to determine the controverted issues, and if the sentence does not decide them in a very specific and positive manner, confusion may ensue and the work of the tribunal will prove futile. Hence the court should exactly determine, as the nature of the case requires, the consequences of its judgment. Effects of a condemnatory sentence upon the defendant should be clearly and specifically indicated. The sentence should state precisely what he is to do, what he is to refrain from doing, what indemnity is to be made, the nature and extent of a penalty, and the manner, time and place of fulfilling the provisions of the sentence. Also, it may be that the sentence should settle other pertinent matters which belong to the controversy. Damages which occurred to the innocent party during the trial, and even before the trial when there was bad faith, are to be recompensed by the guilty party, and fruits and profits arising in the same period from the litigated thing are to be assigned.[7] The petitioner or *actor*

[6] *Cf.* Roberti, *De Processibus*, n. 456; Coronata, *Institutiones Iuris Canonici*, n. 1404.

[7] Roberti, *op. cit.*, n. 456.

cannot be condemned in the sentence unless an exception or countersuit is instituted by the defendant; in which case the plaintiff becomes the defendant and as such may be condenmed.[8] Obscurity and uncertainty in the sentence will, if they make it impossible of execution, render the sentence invalid.[9]

The solution of a controversy may at times be best effected by the use of a conditional sentence, *i. e.*, one whose provisions become operative upon the fulfillment of a certain condition. Such sentences should be used cautiously because they may give rise to complications or leave the controversy in suspense. Unless the condition is intrinsic to the sentence, the controversy will scarcely ever be satisfactorily determined and the sentence is generally to be considered null.[10] However, even an extrinsic future condition will not invalidate a sentence so long as the sentence is not uncertain and obscure.[11] It is not the condition, but the obscurity or uncertainty which it induces, that renders the sentence invalid. Therefore, in giving a conditional sentence, the condition must be such that it can be quickly fulfilled and will preclude any further controversy.[12] An alternative sentence, *i. e.*, one allowing the defendant the right of choice within certain specific limitation, may be imposed at times, and may offer a very practical solution. To be valid, it must not be obscure or uncertain.

§ 2. *Motivation*

Canon 1873, § 1. Sententia debet:

n. 3. Continere rationes seu *motiva* quae dicuntur, tam in facto quam in iure, quibus dispositiva sententiae pars innititur.

§ 2. In tribunali collegiali motiva ab extensore desu-

[8] Coronata, *op. cit.*, n. 1403.

[9] Reiffenstuel, *Ius Canonicum Universum,* II, t. 27, n. 87-91.

[10] *Cf.* Eichmann, *Das Prozessrecht des Codex Iuris Canonici,* p. 175; Coronata, *op. cit.*, n. 1403.

[11] Schmalzgrueber, *Ius Ecclesiasticum Universum,* II, t. 27, n. 39.

[12] Wernz-Vidal, *De Processibus,* n. 592; Lega, *De Iudiciis Ecclesiasticis,* I, n. 608.

mantur ex iis quae singuli iudices in discussione attulerunt, nisi ab ipsa iudicum maiore parte praefinitum fuerit quaenam sint motiva proferenda.

Motivation of the sentence is the inclusion of the reasons or motives upon which the disposition of the controversy is made. Although the sentence does not draw its force from the motives, nevertheless the statement of the motives is conducive to the proper administration of justice and to the development of jurisprudence and also tends to confirm the parties in their trust in the justice of the sentence.[13] The motives *in iure* are the general and particular laws, the juridic principles, and also the sound opinions of canonists, which are brought into the solution of a controversy. Since these motives *in iure* are to be applied to a concrete cause, there arise the motives *in facto,* which are the reasons for applying the provisions of law in a specific way to the cause.[14] The omission of the motives invalidates the sentence.[15] The invalidity is remediable (*sanabilis*), and therefore when the motives are supplied by the judges, the sentence is validated. Sentences handed down by the Signatura are valid, even though not motivated.[16] This is a change from previous prescription.[17]

In stating the motives *in iure,* the judge is free to choose those provisions of law, which he deems pertinent to the cause. He is obliged in no way to use those presented by the parties, the defender of the bond, or the promoter of justice. The motives *in facto* are to be drawn from the facts of the cause (*ex actis et pro-*

[13] Roberti, *op. cit.*, n. 456.

[14] Coronata, *op. cit.*, n. 1403.

[15] Canon 1894, n. 2—"Sententia vitio sanabilis nullitatis laborat quando: Motivis seu rationibus decidendi est destituta. . . . " Rule 182—"Sententia definitiva nulla est, si rationes tam in facto, quam in iure non contineat (Canon 32, § 3, Les propria)"—*Regulae servandae in iudiciis apud S. R. Rotae Tribunal.*

[16] Canon 1605, § 1. "Supremi Tribunalis Signaturae sententiae suam vim habent, quamvis rationes in facto et in iure non contineat."

[17] *Appendix, Ad Regulas Servandas in iudiciis apud Supremum Signaturae Apostolicae Tribunal,* Tit. II, Art. 30.

batis) and their correlation with the provisions of law according to the conscientious judgment of the judge.[18]

When the controversy is based upon or consists of a number of specific points, then each disposition in the sentence on one of these points is to be motivated. The motivation of some of the dispositions may be implicitly contained in that stated for other dispositions; this then will suffice.[19] The points of controversy should be disposed of in systematic manner, which usually can be determined by the natural sequence of their relations with one another. The judge cannot apply another sentence passed by himself or another judge, nor can he concede the conclusions or arguments proposed at the trial; but from these he may draw his own arguments for his decision.[20] Precaution must be used by the judge in seeking the true juridic basis for his judgment, so that he is not unduly influenced by the proficiency or deficiency of the legal reasonings of the parties to the controversy.[21] Reasons for the acceptance or rejection of a part or of the whole of expert testimony is to be recorded in the sentence.[22] If in the enumeration of the motives *in iure* there is an evident and certain error against the provisions of law and the erroneous motives are the sole basis of the decision, then the sentence is invalid.[23] If an error is made in the motives *in facto,* the sentence will be unjust but not *per se* invalid; recourse may be had by appeal or by request for *restitutio in integrum.*[24]

In stating the motives *in iure* and *in facto* for the disposition of a controversy made by a collegiate tribunal, the *relator* is not free to follow any personal choice. His enumeration is always limited to those motives proposed by the judges in support of their

[18] *Cf.* Roberti, *op. cit.*, n. 456.

[19] Roberti, *op. cit.*, n. 456.

[20] Roberti, *op. cit.*, n. 456.

[21] *Cf.* Wernz-Vidal, *op. cit.*, n. 592.

[22] Canon 1804, § 1. "Iudex non peritorum tantum conclusiones, etsi concordes, sed cetera quoque causae adiuncta attente perpendat."

§ 2. "Cum reddit rationes decidendi, exprimere debet quibus motus argumentis peritorum conclusiones aut admiserit aut reiecerit."

[23] Coronata, *op. cit.*, n. 1403; Reiffenstuel, *op. cit.*, II, t. 27, n. 70-74.

[24] Coronata, *op. cit.*, n. 1403; Eichmann, *op. cit.*, p. 173.

votes.[25] When the judges decide on certain specific motives to be stated in the sentence, the *relator* is obliged to state these. A decision by the judges on the motives to be stated, especially in cases of disagreement, will facilitate the work of the *relator* and it will avert the possible need of revisions when the judges prepare to sign the sentence.

§ 3. *Expenses*

Canon 1873, § 1. Sententia debet:
n. 4. Statuere de litis expensis.

The judicial expenses are the costs of litigating the cause before the court. Costs may be placed in four classes: necessary, for which provision is specifically made in the law; useful (*utiles*), those which facilitate the trial but are not considered in the law; immoderate (*voluptuariae*), which are for helpful extravagances; purely superfluous (*mere superfluae*), which are not of utility to the cause.[26] Ordinarily only the necessary costs are to be imposed upon the parties in the sentence. However, the judge may with reason impose also the useful and immoderate costs, but not the purely superfluous costs.[27] As a rule it seems that the useful and immoderate costs should be borne by the parties who avail themselves of the extra service, *e. g.*, of two or more advocates. The fixed amount for the various fees of the court is to be decided by the regulations of the provincial councils, or by the conference of the bishops.[28] In the absence of these, the fees are to be determined by custom or at the discretion of the Ordinary. A deposit in advance to secure payment of the court expenses may be demanded of the plaintiff by the judge; the same may be demanded from the defendant to secure payment of the costs of witnesses and experts, whom he requests to be summoned.[29] The judicial expenses include

[25] *Cf.* Canon 1873, § 2.

[26] Coronata, *op. cit.*, n. 1430; Muniz, *Procedimientos Eclesiasticos*, III, n. 458; *cf.* Wernz-Vidal, *op. cit.*, n. 643.

[27] Muniz, *op. cit.*, n. 460; Coronata, *op. cit.*, n. 1430.

[28] Canon 1909, § 1.

[29] *Cf.* Canons 1909, § 2; 1631, 1788.

three divisions of costs: first, the tax for the support of the tribunal; secondly, the remuneration for the assisting court officials (*notarii, cancellarii,* etc), and the costs of witnesses and experts; thirdly, the remuneration for advocates and procurators.[30]

The general rule for imposing the costs of the trial is that they are to be paid by the party who is the cause of the litigation. The loser in the trial is rightly considered to have caused the litigation and regularly is held to pay the costs.[31] When either party litigates foolishly, this party moreover is to be ordered to repair any damages suffered by the other party.[32] If the responsibility for the litigation falls on both parties, then the costs are to be divided between them in proportion to their responsibility.[33] In renouncing an instance, the party renouncing is to pay the expenses.[34] In an action for the declaration of one's rights, *e. g.*, matrimonial causes, if the defendant did not occasion the litigation, the petitioner is to pay the expenses because he is considered the cause of the trial.[35] A revision or reversal of the sentence in the court of appeal changes accordingly the imposition of costs for the first instance, so that the ultimate loser is to pay the costs of both instances. An appeal from the sentence on the principal cause implicitly contains an appeal from the costs.[36]

Exceptions to the general rule are admitted for several reasons: (*a*) If the controversy is between relations by blood or marriage, the expenses may be portioned to preserve domestic harmony.[37] (*b*) If the question is difficult to decide, a just solution may be a division of expenses.[38] (*c*) In case of abatement of the cause, the expenses are to be divided.[39] (*d*) In case of contempt of court by

[30] Roberti, *op. cit.*, n. 536; *cf.* Appendix de taxatione expensarum iudicialium —*Lex Propria S. R. Rotae et Signaturae Ap.*

[31] *Cf.* Canon 1910, § 1.

[32] *Cf.* Canon 1910, § 2.

[33] Roberti, *op. cit.*, n. 532; *cf.* Canon 1911.

[34] Canon 1741.

[35] Roberti, *op. cit.*, n. 532.

[36] *Cf.* Canon 1913, § 2.

[37] *Cf.* Canon 1911.

[38] *Cf.* Canon 1911.

[39] Canon 1739.

both parties, both are obliged to bear the expenses *in solidum.*[40] (*e*) For any grave and just reason, the judge can impose the cost in part or in whole according to his discretion.[41] (*f*) In case of a friendly agreement by the parties, the expenses are to be imposed according to the agreement.[42] Besides the parties to the controversy, others may be condemned to pay expenses for any act or part of the trial, for which they are responsible.[43]

In criminal causes the general principle of imposing costs on the party causing the trial is in effect. This is explicitly enunciated in the Rules of the Rota:

> In causa criminali qui condemnationem patitur, expensas iudiciales solvere debet, excepto casu quo reo per ipsam condemnationem subtrahantur fructus omnes beneficiales, aliique reditus eidem aliunde non suppetant.[44]

Hence in criminal procedure the defendant, if condemned, is considered the cause of the litigation and is to pay the costs unless he is unable to do so.

Some authors [45] hold that criminal causes are prosecuted for the sake of public good and that therefore all expenses should not be imposed upon the condemned party, but only those for advocates, experts, and other work required by the party. No restriction is made either in the Code or in the Rules of the Rota and, therefore, all judicial expenses may be imposed upon a party condemned in a criminal trial.

Canon 1873, n. 4, prescribes that the expenses of the trial are to be imposed in the sentence. Hence the judges are to decide and specify *which party, or whether both,* should bear the expenses. Generally the sentence only indicates the party. The specified account of the expenses is sent to that party by the notary, after the

[40] Canon 1851, § 2.

[41] Canon 1911.

[42] Canon 1928, § 2.

[43] Roberti, *op. cit.*, n. 533; *cf.* Canons 1644, § 3; 1666, 1766, § 2; 1798.

[44] *Regulae servandae in iudiciis apud S. R. Rotae Tribunal,* § 185, n. 5.

[45] Coronata, *op. cit.*, n. 1430; Noval, *op. cit.*, n. 687; Prümmer, *Manuale Iuris Canonici,* q. 528.

approval of the account by the judges. If the party condemned to the expenses feels himself aggrieved, he may offer protest within ten days to the judge of the same court.[46]

The statement of the sentence imposing the expenses follows the disposition of the controversy. Any form, adding the necessary qualifications, may be used, *e. g.*, "Statuimus praeterea, omnes expensas iudiciales a *N* . . . solvendas esse." The disposition of the expenses may be immediately appended to the disposition of the controversy in the form of a phrase, *e. g.*, "statuentes, etc. . . . "

§ 4. *Gratuitous Legal Service*

The Church, ever solicitous for the poor, has always defended their rights and given them ready access to the justice of her tribunals.[47] In keeping with this tradition, ample provision for free access to the judicial ministrations of ecclesiastical courts is made in the Code. Persons who are unable to pay anything have the right to gratuitous legal service, and those who can pay only a part have a right to a reduction in the expenses.[48] To determine who is entitled to these rights, is left to the discretion of the judge. The poverty of a party need not be absolute; a petitioner in relative poverty is entitled to exemption from all judicial costs.[49] It would seem that a person having means for only the ordinary necessities of life and for reasonable emergencies, *e. g.*, sickness, should be considered relatively poor, and that one having means beyond this but only for a few of the ordinary luxuries of life would be entitled to a reduction. In deciding this matter, specific rules can hardly be definitely determined. It is necessary for the judge to take into consideration national and local conditions, habits and customs of the people. In seeking the gratuitous services of the court or a

[46] Canon 1913, § 1.

[47] C. LXXXIII, Council of Carthage (398)—Mansi, III, 953; C. XI, Council of Toledo (400)—Mansi, III, 1000; c. 11, 15, X, *de foro competenti,* II, 2; c. 26, X, *de verborum significatione,* V, 40.

[48] Canon 1914.

[49] *Cf.* Roberti, *op. cit.*, n. 542; Wernz-Vidal, *op. cit.*, n. 650; Woywod, *A Practical Commentary on the Code of Canon Law,* n. 1831.

reduction in the judicial expenses, the party presents a written request to the judge with documents showing his condition and the amount of his worldly goods, and he also must prove that his litigation is not futile or rash.[50] A letter from the pastor will suffice to determine the financial condition of the party. The judge admits or rejects the request by a decree. In case of refusal of the request, the party may take the matter before the Ordinary or the superior court.[51]

ART. 2. FORM OF THE SENTENCE (CANON 1874)

Canon 1874, § 1. Sententia ferri debet, divino Nomine ab initio semper invocato.

§ 2. Dein exprimat oportet ex ordine qui sit iudex aut tribunal; qui sit actor, reus, procurator, nominibus et domicilio rite designatis, promotor iustitiae, defensor vinculi, si partem in iudicio habuerint.

§ 3. Referre postea debet breviter facti speciem cum partium conclusionibus.

§ 4. Hisce subsequatur pars dispositiva sententiae, praemissis rationibus quibus innititur.

§ 5. Claudatur cum indicatione diei et loci in quibus exarata est et cum subscriptione iudicis vel omnium iudicum, si plures fuerint, et notarii.

The sentence must be drawn up in writing.[52] This is required for validity because a sentence lacking motivation, or the indication of the date and place, or the signatures of the judges and the notary is invalid.[53] The duty of committing the sentence to writing falls to the judge of the single tribunal [54] and to the *relator* in the collegiate tribunal.[55] The following extrinsic elements are to be inscribed in the sentence:

50 *Cf.* Canon 1915, § 1.

51 Roberti, *op. cit.*, n. 543.

52 *Cf.* Canons 1877, 1584, 1872, 1642, § 1.

53 Canon 1894, §§ 2, 3, 4.

54 Canon 1872.

55 Canon 1584.

§ 1. *Divine Invocation*

The invocation of the Divine Name is to be stated at the beginning of the sentence. Some tribunals do not place the invocation here, but immediately before the disposition of the sentence.[56] Other tribunals place an invocation in both places.[57] No specific form is required. The form in common use for the beginning of the sentence is: "In Nomine Dei, Amen." Other forms may be used, *e. g.*, "In Nomine Domini, Amen," "In Nomine Individuae Sanctissimae Trinitatis, Amen." The form "Christi Nomine invocato" appears immediately before the dispositive part of the sentence. The Spanish Rota used "In Nomine Dei, Amen" at the beginning of all sentences, but added "Christi Nomine invocato" before the disposition of only definitive sentences. This serves as a distinction for interlocutory and definitive sentences.[58] The inscription of the Divine invocation into the sentence is not, it seems, necessary for the validity of the sentence.[59]

§ 2. *Identity of the Tribunal and Participants*

After the Divine invocation comes the designation of the tribunal, *i. e.*, the names and surnames of the judges. In the collegiate tribunal there is listed first the name of the *officialis* or presiding judge, then the *relator* and the other collegiate judge or judges. Following these appear the full names and domicile of the plaintiff and defendant with their respective procurators or advocates. The statement of domicile is not required for the decisions of the Roman tribunals.[60] If the defender of the bond or the promoter of justice takes part in the trial, their names are to be included. Particularly should care be taken to designate clearly the parties and their respective advocates, so that no confusion may arise in their regard. Social

[56] Roberti, *op. cit.*, n. 457; *cf. S. R. Rotae Decisiones seu Sententiae.*

[57] El Tribunal de la Rota de la Nunciatura Apostolica—Muniz, *op. cit.*, n. 455.

[58] Muniz, *op. cit.*, n. 181.

[59] Coronata, *op. cit.*, n. 1404.

[60] *Cf. Regulae servandae in iudiciis apud S. R. Rotae Tribunal,* § 181.

status may and, at times, should be mentioned.[61] When the parties have no domicile or quasi-domicile, the place of actual residence is to be given.[62] Indication of the instance the judges are deciding is required.

§ 3. *History of the Cause*

Next is to be stated a brief summary of the cause. This includes the statement of the events or facts leading to the institution of the petition. The object of the petition is set down together with the uncontroverted facts, the issues or doubts of the controversy and the gist of the final plea of the parties.[63] The action of the petitioner and the exception of the defendant are to be clearly defined. The conclusions referred to in Canon 1874, § 3, are the definitive petitions of the final defenses or pleas presented to the court.[64] In a cause being tried in the second instance the tenor of the first sentence is to be stated together with the objective sought by the appellant.

§ 4. *Statement of the Motives*

Paragraph 4 of this canon (1874) prescribes that the sentence be motivated. It does not specify the order of listing the motives. There are indications in the Code [65] from which it might be construed that the motives *in facto* are to precede the motives *in iure*. However, the reverse form is in common use.[66] This seems to be the more practical method, though the order may be changed.[67] The sections of the sentence containing the motives are set off under distinct titles. For the motives *in iure* the title "In iure" is used frequently. Any other appropriate title may be used, *e. g.*, "Ad ius

61 *Cf. Regulae servandae in iudiciis apud S. R. Rotae Tribunal,* § 181, n. 1 a.

62 Roberti, *op. cit.*, n. 457.

63 *Cf.* Canon 1874, § 3; *Regulae servandae in iudiciis apud S. R. Rotae Tribunal,* § 181, n. 1 b.

64 *Cf.* Noval, *op. cit.*, n. 629.

65 Canons 1605, § 1; 1871, § 2; 1873, § 1.

66 *Cf. S. R. Rotae Decisiones seu Sententiae.*

67 Roberti, *op. cit.*, n. 457.

quod attinet," "Ad ius quod spectat," etc. Under the title for the reasons *in iure* are to be stated systematically the relevant provisions of law which enter into the solution of the controversy. The motives or reasons *in facto* are similarly to be expounded under an appropriate title. "In facto" is used frequently;[68] other titles may serve the purpose, *e. g.*, "Ad factum quod attinet," "Ad factum quod spectat," etc. Under the reasons are to be stated the facts with their respective proofs and their correlation with the provisions of law. Listing first the motives *in iure* and then the motives *in facto* fulfills all the elements required by law, and it is recommended for its simplicity and clearness.

The Spanish Rota,[69] which was recently abolished,[70] used a more complex method. Under so many titles of "Resultando" were stated first the facts of the cause, and then under as many titles of "Considerando" the pertinent provisions of law. The first "Resultando" contained the brief historical background of the cause and the substance of the petitions and answers. Each fact of the cause was enumerated successively under its own "Resultando." Each provision of law, each exception and authentic interpretation were inscribed following a "Considerando." Other "Considerandos" were then appended; they contain the correlation of the facts and the provisions of law. The critical study of the evidence was given in one of two methods. The historico-processual method gave the estimation of the proofs under a number of "Considerandos" placed between the "Considerandos" containing the provisions of law and the "Considerandos" containing the correlation of the law and facts. The historico-critical method gave the appraisal of the proofs as they are enumerated under the "Resultandos."

The different methods of the Roman and Spanish Rotas have their own peculiar advantages. That of the Roman Rota gives a simple and clear exposition of the motives *in iure* and *in facto,* which can be understood more readily by a person without legal training. This is effected by a didactic style of explanation of the relevant laws and

[68] *Cf. S. R. Rotae Decisiones seu Sententiae.*

[69] Muniz, *op. cit.*, n. 446-452.

[70] Notification was given to the Bishops of Spain by the Nuntio, 1 Aug., 1933—*Periodica,* XXII (1933), 207.

facts, together with their correlation. In the method of the Spanish Rota there is exposed a single reasoning process through a long grammatical period which develops as it proceeds through the facts (the "Resultandos") and then through the provisions of law (the "Considerandos"). It requires a legally trained mind to follow and to understand the connected thread of juridic reasoning. Muniz holds [71] that this method is more majestic and becomes the dignity of the tribunal. He also declares that the advantage of this method lies in the fact that often it requires greater initiative on the part of the judges to reach through a distinct process of legal logic their conclusions about the facts of the cause, not as they were proposed by the parties, but as they objectively exist. That this statement is true is not at all evident, because the method of the Rota requires equal initiative and legal training on the part of the judges.

The method of the Spanish Rota is generally used in the higher civil courts. The method of the Roman Rota seems to be better adapted for the ecclesiastical courts. It is more direct and more easily understood. There is less danger of becoming involved in technicalities, and the judges are less circumscribed by legal formalities of reasoning in plumbing the depths of difficult obscure issues. While Canon law places due emphasis on proper legal formalities, it does not allow unnecessary processual forms to be so rigid as to become a hindrance to justice. Therefore, in practice, the form of the Roman Rota seems better adapted to most of our lower ecclesiastical courts. Since this form is more easily understood by the parties, it is, also, more satisfactory for them.

§ 5. *Disposition of the Cause*

From the motives *in iure* and *in facto* ensues the judges' decision settling the controversy. The statement of the disposition is absolutely necessary because, if no disposition is made, there is no sentence. The controversy must be definitively decided. When there are several points at issue, a disposition of each is to be stated. The imposition of expenses is set down in this part of the sentence. If

[71] Muniz, *op. cit.*, n. 451.

the case admits, the order of execution of the sentence may be inscribed.[72]

In the Spanish Rota, in introducing the dispositive part of the sentence, there is inscribed the "Visto." It is comprised of the mention of the canons used in the decision and of a reference to the briefs of the defender of the bond or of the promoter of justice, if they participated in the trial. The reference to these briefs is the simple declaration that the decision is given in conformity with the briefs, or that, if not conforming, the decision is given after due consideration of the briefs. An instance of the "Visto" is:

> Visto el canon 1131, de acuerdo con el informe fiscal, Christi Nomine invocato:
> (The disposition is stated here.)

§ 6. *Date, Place and Signatures*

Following the disposition comes the indication of the place and date (day, month and year) and the signatures of the judge, of each judge in the collegiate tribunal, and of the notary. Dissenting judges are obliged to accede to and to sign the majority decision. The dissent is not to be indicated in any manner. If any of the signatures are wanting, the sentence is invalid. The Pontifical Commission declared that a sentence passed by a collegiate tribunal and signed only by the presiding judge and notary was invalid.[73] The same holds for the omission of the date or place. The invalidity in these cases is remediable (*sanabilis*); by supplying the defects the sentence is validated.[74] If the date and place are stated at the beginning of the sentence, they need not be repeated as it suffices to indicate them again, *e. g.*, "Datum die et loco supra dictis." [75]

Art. 3. Form of Interlocutory Sentences (Canon 1875)

Canon 1875. Regulae superius positae locum habent potissimum in proferenda sententia definitiva; sed applicantur etiam, quantum diversa res patitur, in proferenda interlocutoria.

[72] *Cf.* Roberti, *op. cit.*, n. 457.
[73] 14 iul. 1922—*AAS*, XIV (1922), 529.
[74] *Cf.* Canon 1894, n. 3, n. 4.
[75] Muniz, *op. cit.*, n. 445.

§ 1. *Form*

An interlocutory sentence serves to settle some incidental question of considerable moment. It cannot be given without some form of judicial observance, *i. e.*, previous judicial dispute.[76] As to form, Canon 1875 prescribes that the rules laid down in Canon 1874 (*regulae superius positae*) are to be applied to interlocutory sentences to the extent that the different matters permit.[77] With what force this prescription binds, is not explicitly defined. Vidal [78] takes the view that the interlocutory sentence need not be in written form. This is tantamount to withdrawing it completely from the prescription of Canon 1874. Other authors take it as implicitly understood that it is to be drawn up in written form. Thus, Noval [79] declares that it is necessary to have it signed by the judges and notary and to include the indication of date and place. Creusen [80] states that it is to contain a brief narration of the issue and the conclusions of the parties, the inscription of the motives, the indication of the day and the signatures of the judges and notary. Roberti [81] explicitly states that it is to be in written form. Coronata [82] does not seem to insist on the written form. He interprets *regulae superius positae* of Canon 1875 as referring, not merely to Canon 1874, but to all the previous canons on the sentence, and he holds that the rules contained therein do not strictly oblige, though they should generally be observed for prejudicial sentences.

From the foregoing opinions, the more sound conclusion is that the interlocutory sentence should be in writing.[83] In this case it seems that for validity, it should be dated and signed by all of the

[76] Canon 1840. Before the Code an interlocutory sentence did not always require previous judicial dispute; *cf.* De Angelis, *Praelectiones Iuris Canonici*, II, t. 27, c. 2.

[77] Noval, *op. cit.*, n. 630; Vermeersch-Creusen, *op. cit.*, III, n. 232.

[78] Wernz-Vidal, *op. cit.*, n. 587, note 8, n. 3; *cf.* Schmalzgrueber, *op. cit.*, II, t. 27, n. 25; Bouix, *op. cit.*, II, p. 225.

[79] *Op. cit.*, n. 630.

[80] Vermeersch-Creusen, *op. cit.*, III, n. 232.

[81] *Op. cit.*, n. 445.

[82] *Op. cit.*, n. 1402.

[83] *Cf.* Canon 1642, § 1.

judges and the notary. The question is to be briefly indicated together with the reasons supporting the decision. Inclusion of the Divine invocation is appropriate.

An interlocutory sentence may be corrected or revoked *ad instantiam* or *ex officio* at any time before the principal cause is finished.[84] Appeal is admitted only against a prejudicial sentence, *i. e.*, an interlocutory sentence having definitive force.[85]

§ 2. *Formula*

p. ———
N. ——— vs. *N.* ——— (*natura processus*)
n. ———

Sententia Interlocutoria.

In Nomine Dei. Amen.

1. (*Hic habetur brevis relatio quaestionis incidentis agitatae et conclusionum partium.*)

2. (*Hic sequitur motivatio.*)
In iure: . . .

In facto: . . .

3. (*Hic datur pars dispositiva.*)
Quibus omnibus tum in iure cum in facto perpensis, Nos, infrascripti Judices, declaramus: . . .

4. (*Concluditur cum indicatione diei et loci cum subscriptione omnium iudicum et notarii.*)

Art. 4. Publication of Sentence (Canons 1876, 1877)

§ 1. *Time of Publication*

Canon 1876. Sententia, hac ratione redacta, quamprimum publicetur.

[84] Canon 1841.
[85] Canon 1880, n. 6.

Once the sentence is drawn up, it is to be published as quickly as it is deemed possible. This leaves the specific determination of the time of publication to the discretion of the judge, or of the presiding judge in the collegiate tribunal.[86] Coronata [87] interprets *quamprimum* as not permitting delay certainly beyond three days and at most eight days. Muniz [88] allows three days as *tempus utile.* This seems to be a reasonable interpretation, allowing an extension when necessity requires it. This point offers no difficulty, since once the sentence is properly drawn up and signed by the judges, it should be published as quickly as possible. However, no regulation as to the time allowed for drawing up the sentence after reaching the decision is made in the Code.[89] In this case the Rules of the Rota offer a sound norm of procedure:

> Haec [sententia] intra decem dies a decisione edenda est, aut ad summum, intra triginta dies in causis implicatioribus, praesertim ob plura quae proponuntur dubia, et ob copiam documentorum.[90]

Hence, ordinarily it would seem that not more than ten days should elapse from the time the decision is reached until it is published. In the more difficult and complicated causes the limit may be extended to thirty days to give ample time for the judge or the *relator* to draft the sentence.[91] In the tribunal of one judge, drafting the sentence will be less of a task than in the collegiate tribunal, and it seems that the sentence can be drafted, signed and ready for publication on the occasion when the judge makes his decision. Sentences are not to be published on Sundays, holy days of obligation or the last three days of Holy Week, unless necessity, charity or public good require otherwise.[92]

[86] Noval, *op. cit.*, n. 631.

[87] *Op. cit.*, n. 1405.

[88] *Op. cit.*, n. 452.

[89] *Cf.* Canons 1872, 1584.

[90] *Regulae servandae in iudiciis apud S. R. Rotae Tribunal,* § 179, n. 3.

[91] *Cf.* Heiner, *op. cit.*, p. 117; Augustine, *op. cit.*, VII, p. 316; Muniz, *op. cit.*, n. 452.

[92] Canon 1639.

§ 2. *Method of Publication*

Canon 1877. Publicatio sententiae fieri potest tribus modis, vel citando partes ad audiendam sententiae lectionem sollemniter factam a iudice pro tribunali sedente; vel partibus denuntiando sententiam esse penes cancellariam tribunalis, unaque facultatem ipsis fieri eandem legendi et eiusdem exemplar petendi; vel tandem, ubi usus viget, sententiae exemplar transmittendo ad partes per publicos tabellarios ad normam can. 1719.

The publication of the sentence is made *ex officio.*[93] Before the Code the publication was made in the Rota *ad instantiam,* unless the judge was constrained to order it *ex officio* for public good or some other just cause.[94] The publication extends to the interested parties, or their advocates, and the defender of the bond and the promoter of justice when they participate. The Code allows three methods of publication:

First, by citing the parties to hear the sentence solemnly read by the judge sitting in court. This method was followed before the Code.[95] For this method of publication, it seems that the citation of the parties is required for validity, unless the parties are *de facto* present. The presence of the parties is not required provided they have been legitimately cited. The notary is to be present at the publication to record the proceedings in the *acta,* lest any future controversy should arise. It does not seem that the other former conditions of this method are necessary for validity,[96] but only for liceity, viz., that the sentence must be read, read by the judge, and the judge must be seated.[97]

Secondly, by notifying the parties that the sentence is at the chancery of the tribunal and that they can read it there and get

[93] Roberti, *op. cit.,* n. 458.

[94] *Regulae servandae in iudiciis apud S. R. Rotae Tribunal,* § 192.

[95] C. 5, *de sent. et re iud.,* II, 14, in VI°.

[96] *Cf.* Canon 11.

[97] Coronata, *op. cit.,* n. 1405; Augustine, *op. cit.,* p. 316, note 9; *cf.* c. 5, *de sent. et re iud.,* II, 14, in VI°; Reiffenstuel, *op. cit.,* II, t. 27, n. 57 ff.

copies of it. Precaution must be taken to be certain that the parties were actually notified.

Thirdly, by sending, where the custom prevails, a copy of the sentence to the parties by registered mail requiring a receipt from the parties to be returned through the postal service. This method is practical and reliable in this country. If this method is not customary in some place and the two other methods present any difficulty, the Ordinary may introduce its use.[98] The services of a messenger may be used to deliver a copy of the sentence to the parties. Grave caution is to be taken to see that he is reliable. Usually couriers of the court (*cursores*) should be appointed for this work.[99] The notary or some other court official may perform this service; at least, only a trustworthy messenger may be used.[100]

The date of publication for these three methods is recorded as: the day of pronouncement for the first; and the day of mailing or dispatching for the second and third.[101] The reason for recording the date of publication in this manner is that there should be a definite date of publication. Some authors [102] would record the date for the second and third methods as the date of receipt of the notification or copy of the sentence. If this was followed, it is possible that there would be several dates of publication when the parties live in various localities, *e. g.*, one date for the defender of the bond, another for one of the parties, and still a third for the other party. The period of time for appeal is computed from the date of pronouncement for the first method, and from the date of receipt of the notification or copy of the sentence for two other methods.[103] The dates of publication and receipt of the notifications or copies of the sentence by all of the interested participants are to be recorded in the *acta*.

[98] Coronata, *op. cit.*, n. 1405.

[99] *Cf.* Canon 1591, § 1.

[100] *Cf. S. R. Rotae Decisiones seu Sententiae* (1922), dec. VII, n. 3; Wernz, *op. cit.*, V, n. 151, note 93.

[101] *Cf. S. R. Rotae Decisiones seu Sententiae* (1922), dec. VII, n. 2.

[102] Roberti, *op. cit.*, n. 458.

[103] *Cf. S. R. Rotae Decisiones seu Sententiae* (1922), dec. VII, n. 2; Connolly, *op. cit.*, p. 103.

CHAPTER VIII

REMEDIES AGAINST THE SENTENCE

ART. 1. NOTIONS

WHILE the pronouncement of the sentence officially applies to law and effects a legal solution to the controversy of the parties, it does not of itself contain any absolute finality. The law recognizes certain remedies against the sentence, so that the sentence is said to be stable until the remedies are applied. Absolute finality is attained only when legal remedy is no longer applicable.[1] The parties may, and often do, accept the sentence as final; still it is their right to seek a legal remedy against the sentence. The remedies are definitely stated in the Code.

A legal remedy against the sentence is a safeguard granted by law, of which the parties may avail themselves as a means of protection against injury from the actions or omissions of the judges, or from their own ignorance or negligence.[2] The remedies are either ordinary or extraordinary. The ordinary remedy is appeal [3] because of the scope of its application against the sentence. It is a right granted to all parties of the trial who feel that the sentence is unjust, and it extends to all defects in the sentence. The extraordinary remedies are *querela nullitatis, opposito tertii* and *restitutio in integrum;* these are limited in scope to certain persons or to certain conditions,[4] because they are directed against specific defects. Correction of material errors in the sentence is considered under the remedies against the sentence; it is not in a strict sense a remedy of law properly so called.[5] The treatment here on the legal remedies against the sentence will be very brief as it is not given professedly as a part of this dissertation. They are treated because of their connection with the sentence.

[1] Noval, *op. cit.*, n. 633; Roberti, *op. cit.*, n. 459.

[2] *Cf.* Noval, *op. cit.*, n. 633; Wernz, *op. cit.*, V, n. 689.

[3] Canon 1905, § 1.

[4] Roberti, *op. cit.*, n. 461.

[5] Wernz-Vidal, *op. cit.*, n. 597; Coronata, *op. cit.*, n. 1406.

Art. 2. Correction of the Sentence

Material error which may occur in the drafting of the sentence but in no way affecting the judgment, may be corrected by the judge issuing the sentence. The judge must be responsible for the error. The error may arise in transcribing the dispositive part of the sentence, in relating the facts or petitions of the parties or the calculations.[6] This enumeration is not *taxative;* and it seems that any material error in the motivation or in other parts of the sentence may be corrected.[7] In errors of omission which render the sentence remediably invalid, the remedy to be applied is *querela nullitatis.*[8] The correction is brought about *ad instantiam.* Parties desiring the correction petition the judge, who notifies the other party. If there is no objection, the judge then orders a decree of correction.[9] If the other party objects, then the issue is treated as an incidental question which is decided by a decree without observing judicial form of dispute; the decree is appended to the foot of the corrected sentence.[10] In causes involving public welfare the judge can *ex officio* correct the sentence by a decree.[11] The Code defines no time limit for the correction, but it is evident that the correction will usually take place between the publication and the execution of the sentence.

Art. 3. Appeal

§ 1. *Notions*

The most common remedy against the sentence is an appeal,[12] which is the legal right of having a new investigation of the cause before a higher tribunal.

[6] Canon 1878, § 1.

[7] Roberti, *op. cit.*, n. 464.

[8] *Cf.* Canons 1894 ff.

[9] Canon 1878, § 2.

[10] Canon 1878, § 3.

[11] Canons 1618, 1897, § 2.

[12] Canons 1879-1891. For a thorough and scholarly treatment of this subject the reader is referred to "*Appeals*," by Connolly, Washington, D. C., 1932.

> Appellatio hodie non amplius intelligitur ut querela contra iudicem inferiorem, sed potius tamquam petitio ut causa novo et pleniori examini subiiciatur. Unde iudex superior quamvis dicatur sententiam praecedentis instantiae confirmare aut reformare, revera in ius controversum directe pronuntiat.[13]

The purpose of the appeal is to assure a more perfect administration of justice which may be attained by the new investigation, so that errors which may have been made by the lower tribunal can be corrected by this means.[14] The new investigation may be more thorough when new evidence is admitted according to the prescriptions of Canon 1891, § 2. Appeal is directed against a valid but unjust sentence. It may be instituted by a party who feels injured by the sentence, or by the defender of the bond or the promoter of justice, if they participate in the trial. Both parties may appeal if both feel injured. They intend the appeal in their own defense; the promoter of justice and the defender of bond appeal in defense of the public good. Parties may renounce the right of appeal but the defender of the bond or the promoter of justice may be obliged to appeal.[15] The appeal must be made within ten days (*tempus utile*) after the publication of the sentence.[16] The time is computed according to Canon 34, § 3, n. 3. If the exact time of notification does not coincide with the beginning of the day, *i. e.*, midnight, then the day on which the sentence was published does not count in the computation which extends to the tenth full day on which the litigant could exercise his right of appeal.[17]

§ 2. *Cases in Which Appeal Is Not Admitted*

Appeal is not admitted in the following cases:[18]

[13] Roberti, *op. cit.*, n. 58; *cf. Ibid.*, n. 468.

[14] Coronata, *op. cit.*, n. 1408.

[15] Coronata, *op. cit.*, n. 1409; Wernz, *op. cit.*, V, 693; *cf.* Canon 1986.

[16] *Cf.* Canon 1881.

[17] Connolly, *op. cit.*, p. 107; *cf.* Michiels, *op. cit.*, II, pp. 155-160; Cicognani, *Ius Canonicum*, II, p. 195.

[18] Canon 1880.

(1) From the sentence of the Supreme Pontiff himself or the Signatura.

(2) From the sentence of a judge delegated by the Holy See to judge a cause with the clause "appellatione remota."

(3) From a sentence with an invalidating defect.

(4) From a sentence which has become *res iudicata.*

(5) From a definitive sentence which is based on a decisive oath. This restriction includes cases where the cause is settled by agreement [19] or by renouncing the action.[20]

(6) From the decree of a judge or from an interlocutory sentence which does not have definitive force, unless the appeal is joined with an appeal from the definitive sentence.

(7) From a sentence in a cause in which the law demands that the matter must be most speedily settled.

(8) From a sentence against a person guilty of contempt of court who has not retracted his contumacy.

(9) From a sentence against a person who has expressly stated in writing that he renounced his right of appeal.

The foregoing enumeration is *taxative,* and it contains the only sentences excepted from the remedy of appeal.[21]

§ 3. *The Appellate Sentence*

Although the appellate judge is said to confirm or reverse the previous sentence, it is more correct to say that he directly pronounces on the merits of the cause. The appellate sentence must conform to the petition of appeal and no new cause is to be admitted.[22] The judge can reject facts accepted in the previous sentence, or he can accept previously rejected facts; the same can be done in regard to the exceptions. If the sentence was appealed only in part, the appellate sentence is not to pronounce on other parts which were not at least implicitly contained in the title of appeal.[23] The titles not

[19] Canons 1925 ff.

[20] Canons 1740 ff.; Vermeersch-Creusen, *op. cit.,* III, n. 238.

[21] Connolly, *op. cit.,* p. 88; Vermeersch-Creusen, *op. cit.,* III, n. 238.

[22] Canon 1891, § 1.

[23] Canon 1887, § 3; Roberti, *op. cit.,* n. 485.

contained in the appeal become *res iudicata* and the execution of them can be demanded of the lower court.[24] In passing sentence the superior court observes the prescriptions of Canons 1868-1877 on the sentence. If the sentence of the lower court was appealed without any limitation the issue of doubt is proposed as follows: "An sit confirmanda vel reformanda sententia Revmi Tribunalis . . .", or "An sit confirmanda vel infirmanda sententia *etc.* . . ." The sentence is sent to the lower court where, if it confirms the first sentence and becomes *res iudicata,* provision is made for its execution. If it reverses the first sentence, then it is subject to further appeal and does not become *res iudicata* until the time for appeal has elapsed without appeal being made.[25]

Art. 4. *Querela Nullitatis*

§ 1. *Notions*

Querela nullitatis is a remedy by which it is petitioned that the sentence be declared null because of some substantial defect.[26] The defect is extrinsic to the sentence. *Querela nullitatis* may be instituted by the parties and, if participating, by the defender of the bond and the promoter of justice; the judge can *ex officio* within the stated term reveal nullifying defects of the sentence, in which case he then proceeds to correct the sentence.[27] In causes of private good the judge cannot retry the cause independent of the will of the parties.[28]

§ 2. *Irremediably Invalid Sentences*

The Code [29] enumerates the following cases of irremediably invalid sentences:

(1) When the sentence has been passed by an absolutely incom-

[24] Muniz, *op. cit.*, III, n. 472; Coronata, *op. cit.*, n. 1416.
[25] *Cf.* Connolly, *op. cit.*, p. 184.
[26] Noval, *op. cit.*, n. 657.
[27] Canon 1897, §§ 1, 2.
[28] Roberti, *op. cit.*, n. 498.
[29] Canon 1892.

petent judge, or without the legitimate number of judges prescribed by Canon 1576, § 1. In the latter case it seems that only the acts pertaining to the integral tribunal are null, and that these can be renewed by a properly constituted tribunal if the cause has otherwise been properly tried and no further investigation is to be made.[30]

(2) If one of the parties has no juridic standing in court.

(3) If someone has acted in the name of another without a legitimate mandate.

In these cases the *querela nullitatis* can be instituted as an action within thirty years from the date of publication of the sentence; it can be proposed as an exception *in perpetuum*.[31] The petition is made to the tribunal which passed sentence.[32] Excepting possibly the case of an illegal number of judges, when a sentence is irremediably invalid a complete retrial is required for a new sentence. If the sentence is invalid because the required number of judges is lacking, then only those judicial acts are null which must be performed by the whole collegiate tribunal.[33] Hence it seems that after supplying the defect in the number of judges only the passing of a new sentence is required when all the other judicial acts have been properly performed.

§ 3. *Remediably Invalid Sentences*

The Code[34] lists the following cases of remediably invalid sentences:

(1) If there was lacking the proper citation. This is considered to be the citation introducing the cause.[35] The appearance of the parties without being cited would supply the legitimate citation.[36]

(2) If the sentence is not motivated (excepting sentences of the Signatura). Evidently insufficient motives are considered as equiva-

[30] Muniz, *op. cit.*, III, n. 502.
[31] Canon 1893.
[32] Noval, *op. cit.*, n. 660.
[33] Coronata, *op. cit.*, n. 1418.
[34] Canon 1894.
[35] Roberti, *op. cit.*, n. 489.
[36] Canon 1711, § 2.

lent to no motivation.[37] When the motives are stated but erroneous deductions are made the remedy is to be sought either in appeal or *restitutio in integrum*.[38]

(3) If the sentence lacks any of the required signatures, *i. e.*, of each judge and the notary.

(4) If there is lacking the indication of the day, month, year, or the place in which it was given. The defect of any one of these indications invalidates the sentence.[39]

In these cases *querela nullitatis* can be made, either together with appeal within ten days, or separately and by itself within three months from the day of publication to the tribunal which passed the sentence. The citation mentioned in Canon 1894, n. 1, offers a difficulty. Roberti,[40] Coronata[41] and Noval[42] consider it to be the citation which is required at the beginning of the trial according to Canons 1711 ff. If this be the case, then why is the lack of citation called a *remediable* defect. When the citation which is required at the beginning of trial is deficient, then there is no defect in the sentence to be remedied because all of the acts of the process are null and there is no sentence.[43] Could Canon 1894, n. 1, possibly refer to the citation required in the formal pronouncing of the sentence according to Canon 1877? In this case the defect of the citation would come under the terms of Canon 1894, *i. e.*, it would be a *remediable* defect. For the two other methods of publication allowed by Canon 1877, the receipt of the notification or the copy of the sentence would be considered equivalent to citation. These defects in the sentence would be remediable so that the sentence could be validated by supplying them. If the citation mentioned refers to that required at the beginning of trials, it would be more appropriately classified as an *irremediable* defect. When this defect occurs, the whole process

[37] Roberti, *op. cit.*, n. 489.

[38] Coronata, *op. cit.*, n. 1418; Muniz, *op. cit.*, n. 503; Roberti, *op. cit.*, n. 489.

[39] Roberti, *op cit.*, n. 489.

[40] *Op. cit.*, n. 489.

[41] *Op. cit.*, n. 1418.

[42] *Op. cit.*, n. 661.

[43] *Cf.* Canon 1723.

must be renewed. In regard to the other defects mentioned in Canon 1894, when the defect is supplied, the sentence is validated and is to be published.

§ 4. *Extension of "Querela Nullitatis"*

The question is raised as to whether or not the enumeration of invalid sentences in Canons 1892 and 1894 is exclusive so that *querela nullitatis* cannot be applied to sentences which are invalid because of some other processual defect. Coronata,[44] Muniz,[45] Vidal,[46] and d'Angelo [47] consider this enumeration exclusive so that the remedy against other processually defective sentences is *restitutio in integrum*. Roberti [48] maintains that this enumeration is not exclusive so that sentences which are null because of some other processual defect of either positive or natural law, may be opposed by *querela nullitatis*. He lists a number of such invalidating defects, among which is to be found the absence of the defender of bond from a matrimonial cause. This invalidating defect is expressly mentioned by the Signatura.[49] According to Roberti such an invalidating defect is to be attacked by *querela nullitatis*. He applies this remedy to all sentences which are given contrary to invalidating processual laws [50] until prescription excludes it after thirty years.[51] *Restitutio in integrum* is a remedy applied against an evident injustice in a sentence which is *res iudicata* and does not admit of appeal or *querela nullitatis*.[52] A sentence may contain a processual defect and nevertheless be just. In case a sentence contains an invalidating processual defect the proper remedy against it seems to be *querela nullitatis*. Hence the writer follows the opinion of Roberti with the same qualification which he makes:

[44] *Op. cit.*, n. 1418.

[45] *Op. cit.*, III, n. 505.

[46] Wernz-Vidal, *op. cit.*, n. 623.

[47] *Periodica*, XVIII (1929), 37 ff.

[48] *Op. cit.*, n. 491 ff.

[49] *AAS*, XI (1919), 295 ff; *cf. Apollinaris*, I (1928), 108.

[50] *Op. cit.*, n. 523; *Apollinaris*, II (1929), 476 ff.

[51] *Op. cit.*, n. 494.

[52] *Cf.* Canon 1905, § 1.

"... salva meliore iudicio, et salva auctoritate iurisprudentiae superiorum tribunalium vel Commissionis erectae ad Codicem interpretandum. . . ."

Art. 5. The Opposition of a Third Party

Oppositio tertii is a remedy granted to persons who fear injury to their rights from the prescription of a definitive sentence, so that they may attack and oppose the execution of the sentence.[53] While a third party can institute a new process to defend his rights, *oppositio tertii* is quicker, more convenient and equally effective. A third party may also defend his rights by intervention in the process before the conclusions of the cause.[54] *Oppositio tertii* may be proposed to the judge who passed the sentence or it may be made by appealing to the superior court.[55] The petition is to be made before the execution of the sentence;[56] after the execution of the sentence the remedy is to be had by instituting a new process.[57] When *oppositio tertii* is instituted by way of appeal, the ten day time limit does not apply so long as the sentence has not been executed.[58] Canon 1900 states that the laws governing appeal are to be observed after the admission of the instance (*admissa instantia*). Hence before the admission of the instance, they do not apply. The third party must propose the remedy. He must prove, either a certain injury of his rights caused by the sentence itself, or a probable injury arising from the execution of the sentence which will be gravely prejudicial to him.[59] If neither condition is proved, the judge rejects the petition by a decree containing the reasons in fact and in law; he then proceeds with the execution of the sentence.[60] If the petition is admitted in the

[53] Canon 1898.

[54] Canon 1852, § 2.

[55] Canon 1899, § 1.

[56] Canon 1898.

[57] Roberti, *op cit.*, n. 504.

[58] Coronata, *op. cit.*, n. 1421; Roberti, *op. cit.*, n. 504. Contra Muniz, *op. cit.*, III, n. 510; Wernz-Vidal, *op. cit.*, n. 627.

[59] *Cf.* Canon 1899, §§ 2, 3; Roberti, *op. cit.*, n. 503.

[60] *Cf.* Canon 1899, § 4.

court of appeal the issue is treated according to laws governing appeals; if it is admitted before the judge who passed the sentence, it is treated as an incidental cause.[61] When the proponent of *oppositio tertii* wins his cause, the former sentence is to be revised so as to vindicate his rights.[62]

Art. 6. *Res Iudicata*

A cause irrevocably adjudged, *res iudicata,* is a sentence which has attained that degree of stability that it cannot be oppugned by the ordinary remedy of appeal but only by the extraordinary remedies of *querela nullitatis, oppositio tertii* or *restitutio in integrum.*[63] *Res iudicata* is attained when two conformable sentences have been passed, when no appeal was made or, if made, was not prosecuted within the proper time limit, and when appeal is not allowed.[64]

Causes *de statu personarum* never become *res iudicata.*[65] These are usually enumerated as causes concerning matrimony, ordination, and religious profession.[66] When two conformable sentences have been passed on these causes and appeal is not made within ten days, the sentence becomes *exsecutiva.* Further litigation is not to be admitted unless new and weighty arguments or documents are presented.[67] If petition is made in these causes for a new examination, the petition is presented to the next superior court which alone has jurisdiction to retry the case. In the Rota the petition is presented to a *new turn,* from which, if rejected, petition may be made to the Signatura. New evidence is to be admitted only in the appellate court because a cause adjudicated in one tribunal cannot be tried in another court of similar instance.[68] A new process may be instituted

[61] Canon 1900.

[62] Canon 1901.

[63] Roberti, *op. cit.*, n. 508; Coronata, *op. cit.*, n. 1423; Muniz, *op. cit.*, III, n. 516.

[64] Canon 1902.

[65] Canon 1903.

[66] Noval, *op. cit.*, n. 675; Vermeersch-Creusen, *op. cit.*, III, n. 245; Dec. XIX, n. 4—*S. R. Rotae Decisiones seu Sententiae* (1922).

[67] Canon 1903.

[68] Pont. Comm., 16 iun., 1931, n. 3—*AAS,* XXIII (1931), 353.

in the same tribunal when there is a new objective, or for the same objective but based on a new cause, since a new objective or a new cause produces a new action.[69]

Art. 7. *Restitutio in Integrum*

Reinstatement in former position (*restitutio in integrum*) is a general provision of law instituted to repair grave injury which arises from valid but rescindable acts and cannot be remedied by any ordinary action.[70] Canon 1905, § 1 applies it as an extraordinary remedy against the sentence to repair an evident injustice when appeal or *querela nullitatis* is not applicable. The irrevocably adjudged sentence must manifestly cause the grave injustice. This is considered to exist only in the following cases: first, when the sentence was based on documents which later proved to be false; secondly, when later there are discovered new documents which prove new facts peremptorily demanding a contrary decision; thirdly, when the sentence was passed through fraud by one party to the injury of the other party; and fourthly, when a prescription of law was evidently neglected.[71] This enumeration of conditions for the use of *restitutio in integrum* is *taxative*.[72] Under false documents is included other false proofs, *e. g.*, false testimony, oaths, etc.[73] With revelation of new documents or testimony, *restitutio in integrum* is to be denied unless they decisively require a reformation of the sentence.[74] Whether or not neglect of processual prescriptions of law is included under the fourth condition is disputed. The question is discussed at length by Roberti,[75] and S. d'Angelo.[76] As indicated previously in Article 4, Roberti maintains that processual defects are to be opposed by *querela nullitatis* instead of *restitutio in integrum*. D'Angelo declares that

[69] Roberti, *op. cit.*, n. 513.

[70] Canon 1687; Roberti, *op. cit.*, nn. 249, 514.

[71] Canon 1905, § 2, nn. 1, 2, 3, 4.

[72] Roberti, *op. cit.*, n. 515.

[73] Roberti, *op. cit.*, n. 516; Coronata, *op. cit.*, n. 1427.

[74] *Cf. AAS*, X (1918), 391 ff.

[75] Roberti, *op. cit.*, 519 ff, *Apollinaris*, II (1929), 476 ff.

[76] *Periodica*, XVIII (1929), 37 ff.

processual defects are included under *legis praescriptum* mentioned in Canon 1905, § 2, n. 4, so that *restitutio in integrum* is the proper remedy to be applied against them.

Restitutio in integrum is granted by the judge who issues the sentence except when it is petitioned because of neglect of some prescription of law; in which case the appellate court grants the reinstatement.[77] When a petition for *restitutio in integrum* is made against a sentence of the Rota, the Signatura decides the question of its admission.[78] When *res iudicata* arises from two conformable sentences, Muniz [79] and Vidal [80] hold that petition for *restitutio in integrum* is to be made to the tribunal of the first instance; Roberti [81] and Coronta [82] take the view, which seems to be the more sound, that it is to be made to the tribunal of the second instance.

The process of *restitutio in integrum* has two phases: First, the decision on the question of admitting petition (*iudicium restituens*); and secondly, the pronouncement on the merits of the cause (*iudicium restitutorium*). Both questions may be tried at the same time and decided by one sentence under two titles.[83] This sentence is subject to all remedies of law, except perhaps when it conforms perfectly with the previous sentence.[84]

Art. 8. Execution of the Sentence

The execution of the sentence ordinarily does not take place until the ordinary remedies are no longer applicable. Hence Canon 1917, § 1, prescribes that when the sentence becomes *res iudicata,* it can be executed. While a sentence which has become *res iudicata* is still subject to the extraordinary remedies of *restitutio in integrum* and *oppositio tertii,* these remedies do not suspend the execution of

[77] Canon 1906.

[78] Canon 1603, § 1, n. 4.

[79] *Op. cit.,* III, n. 521.

[80] Wernz-Vidal, *op. cit.,* n. 640.

[81] *Op. cit.,* n. 526.

[82] *Op. cit.,* n. 1428.

[83] Roberti, *op. cit.,* n. 525.

[84] Roberti, *op. cit.,* n. 529.

the sentence unless they are instituted before the sentence is executed.[85] When *querela nullitatis* is instituted, it seems that the judge can at his discretion suspend the execution of the sentence.[86] Appeal suspends the execution of the sentence unless the law expressly denies it, except in the case of provisional execution.[87] Some sentences are self-executory and require no order of execution, *e. g.*, absolutory sentences in contentious and usually in criminal causes, sentences inflicting censures.[88]

Provisional execution of the sentence before it becomes *res iudicata* is allowed by Canon 1917, § 2. The use of the provisional execution of the sentence is left to the discretion of the judge when the necessary conditions exist. It may be used in order to make provisions or payments for the necessary maintenance of a party or if some other grave necessity requires it.[89] If the judge orders a provisional execution of the sentence, he is to have sufficient surety to protect the other party in case the execution is revoked. Some authors [90] in interpreting the term *ordinatis* in Canon 1917, § 2, n. 1: "Si agatur de provisionibus seu praestationibus ad necessariam sustentationem ordinatis," as "ordained men," restrict the provisional execution in this case to maintenance of clerics. This interpretation does not seem to be correct.[91]

The execution of the sentence takes place after the issuance of an executory decree by the judge passing sentence. This decree may be issued either separate from the sentence or, if the nature of the cause allows, it may be included in the tenor of the sentence itself.[92] The sentence is to be executed by the Ordinary of the place where the sentence was passed in the first instance, or by his delegate.[93] If the Ordinary refuses or neglects to execute the sentence, the judge of the

[85] Canons 1899, § 4; 1907, § 1.

[86] Roberti, *op. cit.*, n. 547.

[87] Canon 1889, § 2.

[88] Canon 2243, § 1.

[89] Canon 1917, § 2, nn. 1, 2.

[90] Muniz, *op. cit.*, III, n. 527; Eichmann, *op. cit.*, p. 190.

[91] *Cf.* Woywod, *op. cit.*, n. 1833; Roberti, *op. cit.*, n. 546.

[92] Canon 1918.

[93] Canon 1920, § 1.

court of appeals attends to the execution either *ad instantiam* or *ex officio*.[94] Within thirty years after a sentence has been pronounced, parties can institute action (*actio iudicati*) to have sentence executed.[95] If the sentence is manifestly unjust so that *restitutio in integrum* may be granted, the executor can *ad instantiam*, or *ex officio* in causes of public good, suspend the execution of the sentence and remit it to the judge issuing the decree of execution.[96]

[94] Canon 1920, § 2.

[95] Roberti, *op. cit.*, n. 547.

[96] *Cf.* Canon 1921, § 2; Roberti, *op. cit.*, n. 549.

CHAPTER IX

THE SENTENCE IN MATRIMONIAL CAUSES

ART. 1. SOLEMN MATRIMONIAL TRIALS

§ 1. *Competent Forum*

REGULATIONS on competency for matrimonial causes are laid down in Canons 1962 to 1964. The competent court of the first instance, excepting causes reserved to the Holy See, is the court where the marriage was celebrated or the court where the convened party or, if one of the parties is a non-Catholic, where the Catholic party has a domicile or a quasi-domicile.[1] In response to questions on forum of domicile or quasi-domicile the Pontifical Commission [2] declared: that a wife maliciously deserted by her husband was to convene him before the court of his domicile or quasi-domicile; and that a wife not legitimately separated from a non-Catholic husband could convene him in the court of her own quasi-domicile or of the domicile of her husband. An instruction of the Sacred Congregation of the Sacraments [3] declared that in certain contingencies the judge could decide that a matrimonial cause could not be heard in the court of quasi-domicile if there is danger of fraud or error. A recent private decision of the Signatura [4] is to be noted. In a case in which a marriage took place in New York and the husband subsequently maliciously deserted his wife and went to Florence, Italy, where he sought to institute action against the marriage and, being denied, took the case to the Signatura; this Tribunal declared that the Court of Florence was not competent and that the competent court was that of New York. This decision has aroused considerable controversy.[5] In as much as it was made to obviate the danger

[1] Canon 1964; *cf.* Kay, *op. cit.*, p. 90 ff.

[2] 14 iul., 1922, n. 14, ad primum et secundum—*AAS*, XIV (1922), 529.

[3] 23 dec., 1929—*AAS*, XXII (1930), 168; *cf. Periodia*, XIX (1930), 251.

[4] 7 nov., 1932—*Apollinaris*, VI (1933), 102; *Ius Pont.*, XIII (1933), 106.

[5] *Cf. Ius Pont.*, XIII (1933), 232.

of fraud and grave injustice to the deserted party, it is correct and in accordance with the principles enunciated in the instruction of the Sacred Congregation of the Sacraments.[6] However, the arguments adduced are not admissible because they are contrary to the provisions of Canon 1964 and the declarations of the Pontifical Commission.[7] The distinction that the forum of domicile of the convened party was that of the *real* domicile and not the *legal* domicile, is unfounded. To give such an interpretation comes under the authority of the Pontifical Commission and not of the Signatura.

§ 2. *The Sentence*

The sentence in solemn matrimonial trials is to be drawn up according to the norms of Canons 1868 to 1877. From the first sentence of nullity in any instance, the defender of the bond is obliged to appeal.[8] From a second sentence of nullity the defender of the bond of the appellate court may appeal according to his conscientious conviction.[9] If after two sentences for nullity have been pronounced, appeal is not made within ten days, the parties have the right to contract a new marriage[10] The two sentences for nullity must be conformable. The constitution "*Dei Miseratione*"[11] declares that they must be *penitus similes, et conformes.* Hence the nullity of marriage must be established on the same cause in each sentence.[12] It will not suffice to have nullity declared, *e .g.*, by one sentence *ex capite vis et metus* and by the other *ex capite impotentiae.* A sentence contrary to the prescription of Canon 1989, *i. e.*, admitting a cause adjudged in one court in another court of similar instance, is invalid because of absolute incompetency.[13]

[6] 23 dec., 1929—*AAS,* XXII (1930), 168.

[7] 14 iul., 1922, n. 1, n. 14, ad primum—*AAS,* XIV (1922), 526, 529.

[8] Canon 1986.

[9] *Cf.* Canon 1987.

[10] Canon 1987.

[11] 3 nov., 1741—*Fontes,* n. 318.

[12] Cappello, *De Sacramentis,* III, n. 887.

[13] *Apollinaris,* IV (1931), 378; *cf. Pont. Comm.,* 16 iun, 1931, n. 3—*AAS,* XXIII (1931), 353.

§ 3. *Execution of the Sentence*

After the two conformable sentences for nullity have been pronounced and the time for appeal has elapsed, the sentence becomes *exsecutiva* and the appellate court issues an order of execution which is directed to the Ordinary of the place in which the court of first instance sat.[14] The Ordinary then notifies the parties that they have the right to contract legitimately a new marriage. This is not strictly an execution of the sentence because sentences *de statu personarum* do not *per se* require execution; it is rather, an execution of the effects of the sentence. Notification that the marriage has been declared null is to be sent to the pastor of the parish in which the marriage was celebrated and to the pastor of the parishes in which the parties were baptized.[15]

§ 4. *Formula*

p. ....
N.......... vs. *N*..........
Sententia Definitiva — Processus Solemnis Nullitatis Matrimonii
n. ....

TRIBUNAL *N*..........

1. Revmus *N*.........., Officialis (*vel* Praeses), Rev. *N*.........., Relator, et Rev. *N*.........., Iudices, in causa nullitatis matrimonii inter *N*.........., actorem (*domicilium*), repraesentatum per legitimum procuratorem *N*.........., advocatum, et *N*.........., partem conventam, (*domicilium*), repraesentatum per legitimum procuratorem *N*.........., advocatum, interveniente in causa Rev. *N*.........., Vinculi Defensore, sequentem tulerunt in primo gradu definitivam sententiam.
2. (*Hic habentur historia causae, quid petitur a partibus, facta agnita partibus et dubia solvenda*) . . . Omnibus quae de iure erant explenda peractis, quaestio solvenda proponitur sub consueto dubio: "An constat de nullitate matrimonii in casu."

3. (*Hic dantur motiva*)
In Iure:

[14] Laboure-Byrnes, *Procedure in the Diocesan Matrimonial Courts of First Instance*, p. 116.

[15] Canon 1988.

In Facto:

4. (*Hic sequitur pars dispositiva*)
Quibus omnibus tum in iure cum in facto perpensis, Christi nomine invocato, Nos infrascripti iudices, pro Trbunali sedentes, et solum Deum prae oculis habentes, decernimus et definitive sententiamus, ad propositum dubium: "An constat de nullitate matrimonii in casu," Affirmative (*vel* Negative), seu constat (*vel* non constat) de nullitate matrimonii in casu.
Statuimus praeterea expensas iudiciales esse compensandas ab actore (*vel* a parte conventa, *vel* ab utraque parte).
(*Loco*), in Sede Tribunalis, (*die, mense et anno*)

N......................, Officialis (*vel* Praeses)
N......................, Relator
N......................

N......................, Notarius

Art. 2. The Documentary Process

§ 1. *Nature of the Sentence*

Question is raised as to whether or not the documentary process (Canons 1990-1992) is concluded by a true judicial sentence. Solution of this question devolves from the nature of the process itself. The greater number of commentators [16] seem to regard it as an administrative process but for the most part they offer a few arguments for their position and do not extensively define the issue. Gasparri [17] seems to support this view in the phrase: " . . . praetermissis cuiusque generis sollemnitatibus, seu quovis processu iudiciali. . . ." On the other hand Triebs [18] and especially Noval [19] propose very strong and logical arguments for the judicial nature of the process. Kay [20] after thorough examination and reasoning on the

[16] Vlaming, *Praelectiones Iuris Matrimonii,* n. 803; Chelodi, *Ius Matrimoniale,* n. 180; Farrugia, *De Matrimonio,* nn. 164, 379; Wernz-Vidal, *Ius Matrimoniale,* n. 704; Lanier, *Procedure Matrimoniale,* p. 2; Cerato, *De Matrimonio,* n. 169; Payen, *De Matrimonio,* n. 2720; Coronata, *op. cit.,* n. 1501.

[17] *De Matrimonio,* n. 1283.

[18] *Periodica,* XX (1931), pp. 93-107.

[19] *Op. cit.,* n. 873.

[20] *Op. cit.,* pp. 126-136.

question concludes that it is by nature judicial. This view is shared by Connolly [21] and Lydon.[22] Roberti [23] considers it as judicial and states that the declaration of the Pontifical Commission,[24] affirming the necessity of citing the defendant, implicitly indicates that the procedure is judicial, even though restricted to a special method of proof. Cappello [25] calls it a summary process and holds that the declaration of nullity is judicial in a wide sense: " . . . sensu lato, non autem stricto. . . ."

The writer considers the more sound view to be that the process is, at least in a wide sense, judicial. Whence the declaration of nullity will be considered a judicial sentence in a wide sense. However, all the regulations for the sentence prescribed by Canons 1868 to 1877 are not required, but only those which from the nature of the matter and the general principles of law and justice are necessary for validity.[26] Thus the sentence requires a written form with the signatures of the Ordinary or his delegate and the notary, and the indications of the place and date. It seems proper to add the motives *in iure* and *in facto*. Hence the sentence in the documentary process will have substantially the same form as in the solemn process.

Competency will be determined according to the norms of Canon 1964. If the process is administrative, the Ordinary can pass on cases in his own territory and on cases of his subjects anywhere. The citation of the parties and the intervention of the defender of the bond are necessary conditions for validity.[27] The citation required is that which is prescribed at the beginning of all trials.[28]

Two facts must be proved in the documentary process: first, the existence of the impediment; secondly, that no dispensation was granted. The existence of the impediment must be established by certain

[21] *Appeals*, p. 67.

[22] Ayrinhac-Lydon, *Marriage Legislation in the New Code of Canon Law*, p. 362.

[23] *Apollinaris*, IV (1931), 380.

[24] 16 iun., 1931, n. 4, ad secundum—*AAS*, XXIII (1931), 353.

[25] *De Sacramentis*, III, n. 891; *Ius Pont.*, XII (1932), 106 ff.

[26] Cappello, *op. cit.*, III, n. 891.

[27] Canon 1990; *Pont. Comm.*, 16 iun., 1931, n. 4, ad secundum—*AAS*, XXIII (1931), 354; Cappello, *op. cit.*, III, n. 891.

[28] *Apollinaris*, IV (1931), 380; *Ius Pont.*, XI (1931), 255; *cf.* Canons 1711 ff.

and authentic documents which are not open to contradiction or exception.[29] Positive facts are to be established by public documents according to the norm of Canon 1816.[30] Since public documents cannot be had for negative facts, *e. g.*, non-reception of baptism in a case of disparity of cult, attested private documents and even oral testimony can be admitted according to the norms of Canons 1789 and 1974.[31] The second fact requires equal certitude with the first. Unquestionable proof that the impediment was never dispensed or never ceased and that the marriage was never subsequently validated is necessary. This proof is to be had from certain and authentic documents or from other legitimate methods of proof.[32]

§ 2. *Cases to Be Admitted*

Authors [33] generally hold that the seven impediments mentioned in Canon 1990 are *taxative*. Vidal [34] holds that the impediment of age can be included, or that at least, the provisions of Canon 1747, n. 1, can be applied *i. e.*, it can be considered as a notorious fact. Gasparri [35] excludes all other impediments and holds that at most "age" can be considered under Canon 1747, n. 1. If the impediment of age is established in this manner it seems probable that the defender of bond is free from obligation of appealing.[36]

Cappello [37] does not consider the enumeration of impediments as *taxative*. He declares that the impediments of age, legal relationship, public honesty, conjugicide of notoriety of law from a legitimately passed sentence and impotence, if it is certainly established by two conformable sentences, may be treated under the provisions of Canon 1990 when they are proved from certain and authentic documents which are not exposed to contradiction or exception. Excepting the

[29] Canon 1990.
[30] *Apollinaris*, IV (1931), 379; Cappello, *op. cit.*, III, n. 891.
[31] Kay, *op. cit.*, p. 147.
[32] Pont. Comm., 16 iun., 1931, n. 4, ad primum—*AAS*, XXIII (1931), 353.
[33] Gasparri, *op cit.*, n. 1283; Chelodi, *op. cit.*, n. 180; Payen, *op cit.*, n. 2721.
[34] Wernz-Vidal, *Ius Matrimoniale*, n. 704, note 47.
[35] *Op. cit.*, n. 1283.
[36] Payen, *op cit.*, n. 2721, note 1.
[37] *Op. cit.*, III, n. 891.

impediment of impotence, this view may be tenable if Canon 1747, n. 1, is applicable to the case. To admit generally other impediments than those mentioned in Canon 1990, it seems that further declarations from the Holy See would be required.

§ 3. *Non-Catholics as Petitioners*

While the Holy Office [38] declared that a non-Catholic cannot be admitted without its special permission as an *actor* in a matrimonial cause, this declaration does not seem to apply to the documentary process. In applying Canon 1990 no formal plaintiff is required when the marriage is evidently null.[39] Under the old law the inability to be an *actor* in a solemn process, which resulted from heresy or schism, did not exist in the case of the documentary process.[40] This is confirmed since the Code by private rescripts from the Holy See.[41]

§ 4. *Formula for Disparity of Cult Case*

Declaratio
Definitiva

N.............. vs *N*..............
Processus Documentarius
Nullitatis Matrimonii
n. ....

TRIBUNAL *N*.......................

In Nomine Dei. Amen.

1 Revmus *N*........................., Ordinarius (*vel* Iudex delegatus ab Ordinario), in casu nullitatis matrimonii inter *N*......................., (*domicilium*), et *N*........................., (*domicilium*), citatis partibus et interveniente *N*...................., Vinculi Defensore, iuxta normas sacri canonis 1990 sequentem declarationem nullitatis tulit.

2 In Iure: (*Hic adducitur canon ad casum pertinens*)
In Facto: Adsunt documenta certa et authentica:
(1) De baptismo *N*......................

[38] 27 ian., 1928—*AAS*, XX (1928), 75.

[39] Aryinhac-Lydon, *op. cit.*, p. 368.

[40] *AER*, LXXXVI (1932), 69; *cf. Collectanea S. C. P. F.*, n. 1706.

[41] *AER*, LXXXVI (1932), 72.

(2) De divortio civili obtento.

Adsunt probationes pariter certae:

(3) De non-baptismo *N*.................... Testes sequentes, de quorum veracitate ex testimonio authentico parochi *N*.................... (*vel N*...................., *N*....................) constat, auditi sunt: *N*...................., *N*...................., *etc.*

(4) De defectu dispensationis super impedimento.................... ex testimonio Curiae *N*.................... et *N*....................

(5) De non-convalidatione matrimonii, ex testimonio Curiae *N*.................... et *N*....................

3 Quibus omnibus tum in iure cum in facto perpensis, Nos decernimus et definitive declaramus constare de nullitate matrimonii in casu seu matrimonium in casu invalidum ab initio fuisse.

(*Loco, dei, mense et anno.*)

N.................... Ordinarius (*vel* Iudex delegatus ab Ordinario)

N.................... Notarius

BIBLIOGRAPHY

Sources

Acta Apostolicae Sedis, Rome, 1909—

Acta Sanctae Sedis, 41 vols., Rome, 1865-1908.

Appendix, Ad Regulas Servandas in iudiciis apud Supremum Apostolicae Tribunal, Rome, 1915.

Code of Hammurabi, trans. Robert Francis Harper, London, 1904.

Codex Iuris Canonici, Rome, 1929.

Codex Theodosianus, Ed. P. Krueger, Th. Mommsen, P. M. Meyer, 3 vols., Berlin, 1905.

Codicis Iuris Canonici Fontes, cura Emi. Petri Card. Gasparri editi, 6 vols., Rome, 1925-1933.

Collectanea S. Congregationis de Propaganda Fide, 2 vols., Rome, 1907.

Corpus Iuris Civilis, 3 vols., Berlin, 1928-1929. Vol. I: *Institutiones,* recognovit P. Krueger; *Digesta,* recognovit Th. Mommsen, *retractavit* P. Krueger; Vol. II: *Codex Iustinianus,* recognovit et retractavit P. Krueger; Vol. III: *Novellae,* recognovit R. Schoell, opus Schoelli morte interceptum absolvit G. Kroll.

Corpus Iuris Canonici, ed. Richter-Friedberg, 2 vols., Leipzig.

Decretals D. Gregorii IX, una cum Glossis Restitutae, Rome, 1582.

Denziger, H.-Bannwart, C., *Enchiridion Symbolorum Definitionum et Declarationum de Rebus Fidei et Morum,* 14, 15 ed., Freiburg, 1922.

Liber Sextus Decretalium, una cum Clementinis et Extravagantibus earumque glossis restitutis, Rome, 1582.

Mansi, Joannes Dominicus, *Sacrorum Conciliorum Nova et Amplissima Collectio,* 53 vols., Paris, 1901-1927.

Migne, Jacques Paul, *Patrologia Graeca,* 161 vols., Paris, 1858-1864.

Migne, Jacques Paul, *Patrologia Latina,* 221 vols., Paris, 1847-1870.

Regulae Servandae in iudiciis apud S. Romanae Rotae Tribunal, Rome, 1910.

Regulae Servandae in iudiciis apud Supremum Signaturae Apostolicae Tribunal, Rome, 1912.

Sanctae Romanae Rotae Decisiones seu Sententiae, Rome, 1909.

Works of Reference

Aertnys-Damen, *Theologia Moralis,* 2 vols., Turin, 1928.

Alphonsus M. de Ligoria, *Theologia Moralis,* 2 vols., Turin, 1891.

Ayrinhac-Lydon, *Marriage Legislation in the New Code of Canon Law,* New York, 1932.

[Bachofen], Charles Augustine, *A Commentary on the New Code of Canon Law,* 4 ed., 8 vols., St. Louis, 1918-1929.

Berardi, Carolus, *Gratiani Canones,* 4 vols., Venice, 1777.

Blat, Albertus, *Commentarium Textus Codicis Iuris Canonici,* 6 vols., Rome, 1921-1927.

Bouix, D., *Tractatus de Iudiciis Ecclesiasticis,* 2 ed., 2 vols., Paris, 1866.

Calisse, Carlo, *A History of Italian Law,* trans. L. B. Register, Boston, 1928—Vol. VIII of *The Continental Legal History Series,* 10 vols.

Cappello, Felix M., *Summa Iuris Publici Ecclesiastici,* Rome, 1928.

————, *Tractatus Canonico-Moralis de Sacramentis,* 3 vols., Rome, vol. I, 2 ed., 1928, vol. II, 2 ed., 1929-1932, vol. III, 3 ed., 1933.

Catholic Encyclopedia, 15 vols., New York, 1917.

Cerato, Prosdocimus, *Matrimonium a Codice Iuris Canonici integra Desumptum,* Padua, 1927.

Chelodi, Joannis, *Ius de Personis,* 2 ed., Trent, 1927.

————, *Ius Matrimoniale,* 3 ed., Trent, 1921.

Cicognani, Hamletus, *Commentarium ad Librum I Codicis,* 2 vols., Rome, 1925.

Collinet, P., et Gifford, A., *Precis de Droit Romain,* 3 ed., 2 vols., Paris, 1930.

Connolly, Thomas A., *Appeals,* Washington, 1932.

Coronata, Matthaeus a, *De Processibus,* Rome, 1933.

Costa, Emilio, *Profilo Storico del Processo Civile Romano,* Rome, 1918.

D'Angelo, Sosio, *Saggi su Questioni giuridiche,* Turin, 1928.

De Angelis, Philippus, *Praelectiones Iuris Canonici,* 3 vols, Rome, 1878.

Devereux, John C., *The Most Material Parts of Kent's Commentaries,* New York, 1870.

Devoti, Joannis, *Institutionum Canonicarum,* Liege, 1860.

Eichmann, Eduard, *Lehrbuch des katholischen Kirchenrechtes,* Paderborn, 1926.

————, *Das Prozessrecht des Codex Iuris Canonici,* Paderborn, 1921.

Engelmann, Arthur, *A History of Continental Civil Procedure,* trans. R. W. Millar, Boston, 1927—Vol. VII of *The Continental Legal History Series,* 10 vols.

Esmein, A.-Génestal, R., *Le Mariage en Droit Canonique,* Paris, 1929.

Farrugia, Nicolaus, *De Matrimonio et Causis Matrimonialibus,* Rome, 1924.

Ferraris, F. Lucius, *Prompta Bibliotheca Canonica,* 9 vols., Rome, 1885-1892.

Fournier-La Bras, *Histoire des Collections Canoniques en Occident,* 2 vols., Paris, 1931-1932.

Gasparri, Petrus, *De Matrimonio,* 2 vols., Rome, 1932.

Gregory, Donald J., *The Pauline Privilege,* Washington, 1931.

Heiner, F.-Wynen, A., *De Processu Criminali Ecclesiastico,* Ratisbon, 1912.

Hinchius, Paul, *Decretales Pseudo-Isidorianae,* Leipzig, 1863.

Hostiensis (Henricus de Segusia), *Summa Aurea,* Lyons, 1586.

Joyce, George H., *Christian Marriage,* London, 1933.

Kay, Thomas Henry, *Competence in Matrimonial Procedure,* Washington, 1929

Labouré-Byrnes, *Procedure in the Diocesan Matrimonial Courts of First Instance,* New York, 1928.

Lanier, Chanoine Henri, *Guide Pratique de la Procédure Matrimoniale*, Paris, 1927.

Lega, Michael, *De Iudiciis Ecclesiasticis*, 2 vols., Rome, 1896.

Lessius, Leonardus, *De Iustitia et Iure*, Antwerp, 1617.

Lyons, Avitus E., *The Collegiate Tribunal of the First Instance*, Washington, 1932.

Maroto, Philippus, *Institutiones Iuris Canonici*, 2 vols., Rome, 1921.

Michiels, Gommarus, *Normae Generales Iuris Canonici*, 2 vols., Dublin, 1929.

Mommsen, Th., *Le Droit Penal Romain, trans. J. Duquesne*, Vol. I, Paris, 1907.

Muniz, T., *Procedimientos Eclesiasticos*, 3 vols., Seville, 1930.

Noval, Josephus, *De Processibus*, Rome, Vol. I, 1920; Vol II, 1932.

Panormitanus, Abbas (Nicolaus de Tudeschis), *Commentaria in quinque Libros Decretalium*, 8 vols., Venice, 1578.

Payen, G., *De Matrimonio in Missionibus*, 3 vols., Zi-ka-wei, 1929.

Pirhing, Enricus, *Ius Canonicum in V Libros Decretalium*, 4 vols., Venice, 1759.

Prümmer, Dominicus, *Manuale Iuris Canonici*, Freiburg, 1927.

Reiffenstuel, Anacletus, *Ius Canonicum Universum*, 4 vols., Antwerp, 1743.

Roberti, Franciscus, *De Processibus*, 2 vols., Rome, 1926.

Sanchez, Thomas, *De Sancto Matrimonii Sacramento*, Lyons, 1669.

Santi, Franciscus, *Praelectiones Iuris Canonici*, 2 vols, Ratisbon, 1892.

Savigny, F., *Sistema del Diritto Romano Attuale*, trans. Vittorio Scialoja, Turin, 1896.

Schaefer, Timotheus, *De Religiosis*, 2 ed., Münster, 1931.

Schmalzgrueber, Franciscus, *Ius Ecclesiasticum Universum*, 6 vols., Rome, 1843-1845.

Schmier, Franciscus, *Ius Canonicum Universum*, 2 vols., Venice, 1754.

Sherman, Charles Phineas, *Roman Law in the Modern World*, 2 ed., 3 vols., New Haven, 1922.

Smith, S. B., *Elements of Ecclesiastical Law*, 3 vols., New York, 1882.

Sohm, Rudolph, *The Institutes of Roman Law*, trans. James C. Ledlie, 3 ed., Oxford, 1926.

Thomas Aquinas, *Omnia Opera*, 25 vols., Parma, 1867.

Van Hove, A., *Prolegomena, Commentarium Lovaniense*, Vol. I, Tom. I, Rome, 1928.

——————, *De Legibus Ecclesiasticis, Commentarium Lovaniense*, Vol. I, Tom. II, Rome, 1930.

Vermeersch, A.-Creusen, J., *Epitome Iuris Canonici*, 3 ed., 3 vols., Mechlin, 1927.

Vives, Joannis, *Compendium Iuris Canonici*, 4 ed., 3 vols., Rome, 1905.

Vlaming, Th. M., *Praelectiones Iuris Matrimonii*, Bussum, 1919-1921.

Vromant, G., *De Matrimonio*, Louvain, 1931.

Wernz, Franciscus X., *Ius Decretalium*, 6 vols., 2 ed., Rome, 1905-1913.

Wernz, F. X.-Vidal, Petrus, *De Processibus,* Rome, 1928.
————, *Ius Matrimoniale,* 2 ed., Rome, 1928.
Woywod, Stanislaus, *A Practical Commentary on the Code of Canon Law,* 3 ed., 2 vols., New York, 1929.

Periodicals

American Ecclesiastical Review (*AER*), Philadelphia, 1889—
Apollinaris, Rome, 1928—
Archiv für katholisches Kirchenrecht (*AKKR*), Mainz, 1857—
Ephemerides Theologicae Lovaniensis (*ETL*), Louvain, 1924—
Ius Pontificium, Rome, 1921—
Monitore Ecclesiastico, Il, Rome, 1888—
Nouvelle Revue Theologique (*NRT*), Tournay, 1869—
Periodica de Re Morali, Canonica, Liturgica, Rome, 1912—

Universitas Catholica Americae

WASHINGTON, D. C.

Facultas Juris Canonici

No. 87

1934

ALPHABETICAL INDEX

BIOGRAPHICAL SKETCH

Delisle Antoine Lemieux was born on July 31, 1902, in Encampment, Wyoming. He received his elementary education in public schools of Wyoming and Colorado, and his secondary education in Cathedral High School, Denver. After two years college training at Regis College, Denver, he was admitted to St. Thomas Seminary, Denver, from which he received the degree of Master of Arts. He was ordained December 21, 1926. In September, 1931, he entered the Catholic University of America to pursue a graduate course of studies in the School of Canon Law. On June 15, 1932, he received the degree of Licentiate of Canon Law.

CANON LAW STUDIES

1. Freriks, Rev. Celestine A., C.PP.S., J.C.D., Religious Congregations in Their External Relations, 121 pp., 1916.
2. Galliher, Rev. Daniel M., O.P., J.C.D., Canonical Elections, 117 pp., 1917.
3. Borkowski, Rev. Aurelius L., O.F.M., De Confraternitatibus Ecclesiasticis, 136 pp., 1918.
4. Castillo, Rev. Cayo, J.C.D., Disertacion Historico-canonica sobre la Potestad del Cabildo en Sede Vacante o Impedida del Vicario Capitular, 99 pp., 1919 (1918).
5. Kubelbeck, Rev. William J., S.T.B., J.C.D., The Sacred Penitentiaria and Its Relations to Faculties of Ordinaries and Priests, 129 pp., 1918.
6. Petrovits, Rev. Joseph J. C., S.T.D., J.C.D., The New Church Law on Matrimony, X-461 pp., 1919.
7. Hickey, Rev. John J., S.T.B., J.C.D., Irregularities and Simple Impediments in the New Code of Canon Law, 100 pp., 1920.
8. Klekotka, Rev. Peter J., S.T.B., J.C.D., Diocesan Consultors, 179 pp., 1920.
9. Wannenmacher, Rev. Francis, J.C.D., The Evidence in Ecclesiastical Procedure Affecting the Marriage Bond, 1920. (Not Printed.)
10. Golden, Rev. Henry Francis, J.C.D., Parochial Benefices in the New Code, IV-119 pp., 1921. (Printed 1925.)
11. Koudelka, Rev. Charles, J., J.C.D., Pastors, Their Rights and Duties According to the New Code of Canon Law, 211 pp., 1921.
12. Melo, Rev. Antonius, O.F.M., J.C.D., De Exemptione Regularium, X-188 pp., 1921.
13. Schaaf, Rev. Valentine Theodore, O.F.M., S.T.B., J.C.D., The Cloister, X-180 pp., 1921.
14. Burke, Rev. Thomas Joseph, S.T.B., J.C.D., Competence in Ecclesiastical Tribunals, IV-117 pp., 1922.
15. Leech, Rev. George Leo, J.C.D., A Comparative Study of the Constitution "Apostolicae Sedis" and the "Codex Juris Canonici," 179 pp., 1922.
16. Motry, Rev. Hubert Louis, S.T.D., J.C.D., Diocesan Faculties According to the Code of Canon Law, II-167 pp., 1922.
17. Murphy, Rev. George Lawrence, J.C.D., Delinquencies and Penalties in the Administration and the Reception of the Sacraments, IV-121 pp., 1923.
18. O'Reilly, Rev. John Anthony, S.T.B., J.C.D., Ecclesiastical Sepulture in the New Code of Canon Law, II-129 pp., 1923.
19. Michalicka, Rev. Wenceslas Cyrill, O.S.B., J.C.D., Judicial Procedure in Dismissal of Clerical Exempt Religious, 107 pp., 1923.

20. DARGIN, REV. EDWARD VINCENT, S.T.B., J.C.D., Reserved Cases According to the Code of Canon Law, IV-103 pp., 1924.
21. GODFREY, REV. JOHN A., S.T.B., J.C.D., The Right of Patronage According to the Code of Canon Law, 153 pp., 1924.
22 HAGEDORN, REV. FRANCIS EDWARD, J.C.D., General Legislation on Indulgences, II-154 pp., 1924.
23. KING, REV. JAMES IGNATIUS, J.C.D., The Administration of the Sacraments to Dying Non-Catholics, V-141 pp., 1924.
24. WINSLOW, REV. FRANCIS JOSEPH, A.F.M., J.C.D., Vicars and Prefects Apostolic, IV-149 pp., 1924.
25. CORREA, REV. JOSE SERVELION, S.T.L., J.C.D., La Potestad Legislativa de la Iglesia Católica, IV-127 pp., 1925.
26. DUGAN, REV. HENRY FRANCIS, M.A., J.C.D., The Judiciary Department of the Diocesan Curia, 87 pp., 1925.
27. KELLER, REV. CHARLES FREDERICK, S.T.B., J.C.D., Mass Stipends, 167 pp., 1925.
28. PASCHANG, REV. JOHN LINUS, J.C.D., The Sacramentals According to the Code of Canon Law, 129 pp., 1925.
29. PIONTEK, REV. CYRILLUS, O.F.M., S.T.B., J.C.D., De Indulto Exclaustrationis necnon Saecularizationis, XIII-289 pp., 1925.
30. KEARNEY, REV. RICHARD JOSEPH, S.T.B., J.C.D., Sponsors at Baptism According to the Code of Canon Law, IV-127 pp., 1925.
31. BARTLETT, REV. CHESTER JOSEPH, A.M., LL.B., J.C.D., The Tenure of Parochial Property in the United States of America, V-108 pp., 1926.
32. KILKER, REV. ADRIAN JEROME, J.C.D., Extreme Unction, V-425 pp. 1926.
33. MCCORMICK, REV. ROBERT EMMETT, J.C.D., Confessors of Religious, VIII-266 pp., 1926.
34. MILLER, REV. NEWTON THOMAS, J.C.D., Founded Masses According to the Code of Canon Law, VII-93 pp., 1926.
35. ROELKER, REV. EDWARD G., S.T.D., J.C.D., Principles of Privilege According to the Code of Canon Law, XI-166 pp., 1926.
36. BAKALARCZYK, REV. RICHARDUS, M.I.C., J.U.D., De Novitiatu, VIII-208 pp., 1927.
37. PIZZUTI, REV. LAWRENCE, O.F.M., J.U.L., De Parochis Religiosis, 1927. (Not Printed.)
38. BLILEY, REV. NICHOLAS MARTIN, O.S.B., J.C.D., Altars According to the Code of Canon Law, XIX-132 pp., 1927.
39. BROWN, BRENDAN FRANCIS, A.B., LL.M., J.U.D., The Canonical Juristic Personality with Special Reference to its Status in the United States of America, V-212 pp., 1927.
40. CAVANAUGH, REV. WILLIAM THOMAS, C.P., J.U.D., The Reservation of the Blessed Sacrament, VIII-101 pp., 1927.
41. DOHENY, REV. WILLIAM J., C.S.C., A.B., J.U.D., Church Property: Modes of Acquisition, X-118 pp,. 1927

42. Feldhaus, Rev. Aloysius H., C.PP.S., J.C.D., Oratories, IX-141 pp., 1927.
43. Kelly, Rev. James Patrick, A.B., J.C.D., The Jurisdiction of the Simple Confessor, X-208 pp., 1927.
44. Neuberger, Rev. Nicholas J., J.C.D., Canon 6 or the Relation of the Codex Juris Canonici to the Preceding Legislation, V-95 pp., 1927.
45. O'Keeffe, Rev. Gerald Michael, J.C.D., Matrimonial Dispensations, Powers of Bishops, Priests, and Confessors, VIII-232 pp., 1927.
46. Quigley, Rev. Joseph, A.M., A.B., J.C.D., Condemned Societies, 139 pp., 1927.
47. Zaplotnik, Rev. Ioannes Leo, J.C.D., De Vicariis Foraneis, X-142 pp., 1927.
48. Duskie, Rev. John Aloysius, A.B., J.C.D., The Canonical Status of the Orientals in the United States, VIII-196 pp., 1928.
49. Hyland, Rev. Francis Edward, J.C.D., Excommunication, Its Nature, Historical Development and Effects, VIII-181 pp., 1928.
50. Reinmann, Rev. Gerald Joseph, O.M.C., J.C.D., The Third Order Secular of Saint Francis, 201 pp., 1928.
51. Schenk, Rev. Francis J., J.C.D., The Matrimonial Impediments of Mixed Religion and Disparity of Cult, XVI-318 pp., 1929.
52. Coady, Rev. John Joseph, S.T.D., J.U.D., A.M., The Appointment of Pastors, VIII-150 pp., 1929.
53. Kay, Rev. Thomas Henry, J.C.D., Competence in Matrimonial Procedure, VIII-164 pp., 1929.
54. Turner, Rev. Sidney Joseph, C.P., J.U.D., The Vow of Poverty, XLIX-217 pp., 1929.
55. Kearney, Rev. Raymond A., A.B., S.T.D., J.C.D., The Principles of Delegation, VII-149 pp., 1929.
56. Conran, Rev. Edward James, A.B., J.C.D., The Interdict, V-163 pp., 1930.
57. O'Neil, Rev. William H., J.C.D., Papal Rescripts of Favor, VII-218 pp., 1930.
58. Bastnagel, Rev. Clement Vincent, J.U.D., The Appointment of Parochial Adjutants and Assistants, XV-257 pp., 1930.
59. Ferry, Rev. William A., A.B., J.C.D., Stole Fees, X-107 pp., 1930.
60. Costello, Rev. John Michael, A.B., J.C.D., Domicile and Quasi-Domicile, VII-201 pp., 1930.
61. Kremer, Rev. Michael Nicholas, A.B., S.T.B., J.C.D., Church Support in the United States, VI-136 pp., 1930.
62. Angulo, Rev. Luis, C.M., J.C.D., Legislación de la Iglesia sobre la intención en la applicación de la Santa Misa, VII-104 pp., 1931.
63. Frey, Rev. Wolfgang Norbert, O.S.B., A.B., J.C.D., The Act of Religious Profession, VIII-174 pp., 1931.
64. Roberts, Rev. James Brendan, A.B., J.C.D., The Banns of Marriage, XIV-140 pp., 1931.

65. Ryder, Rev. Raymond Aloysius, A.B., J.C.D., Simony, IX-151 pp., 1931.
66. Campagna, Rev. Angelo, Ph.D., J.U.D., Il Vicario Generale del Vescovo, VII-205 pp., 1931.
67. Cox, Rev. Joseph Godfrey, A.B., J.C.D., The Administration of Seminaries, VI-124 pp., 1931.
68. Gregory, Rev. Donald J., J.U.D., The Pauline Privilege, XV-165 pp., 1931.
60. Donohue, Rev. John F., J.C.D., The Impediment of Crime, VIII-110 pp., 1931.
70. Dooley, Rev. Eugene A., O.M.I., J.C.D., Church Law on Sacred Relics, IX-143 pp., 1931.
71. Orth, Rev. Clement Raymond, O.M.C., J.C.D., The Approbation of Religious Institutes, 171 pp., 1931.
72. Pernicone, Rev. Joseph M., A.B., J.C.D., The Ecclesiastical Prohibition of Books, XII-267 pp., 1932.
73. Clinton, Rev. Connell, A.B., J.C.D., The Paschal Precept, IX-108 pp., 1932.
74. Donnelly, Rev. Francis B., A.M., S.T.L., J.C.D., The Diocesan Synod, VIII-125 pp., 1932
75. Torrente, Rev. Camilo, C.M.F., J.C.D., Las Processiones Sagradas, V-145 pp., 1932.
76. Murphy, Rev. Edwin J., C.PP.S., J.C.D., Suspension Ex Informata Conscientia, XI-122 pp., 1932.
77. MacKenzie, Rev. Eric F., A.M., S.T.L., J.C.D., The Delict of Heresy in its Commission, Penalization, Absolution, VII-124 pp., 1932.
78. Lyons, Rev. Avitus E., S.T.B., J.C.D., The Collegiate Tribunal of First Instance, XI-147 pp., 1932.
79. Connolly, Rev. Thomas A., J.C.D., Appeals, XI-195 pp., 1932.
80. Sangmeister, Rev. Joseph V., A.B., J.C.D., Force and Fear as Precluding Matrimonial Consent, V-211 pp., 1932.
81. Jaeger, Rev. Leo A., A.B., J.C.D., The Administration of Vacant and Quasi-Vacant Episcopal Sees in the United States, IX-229 pp. 1932.
82. Rimlinger, Rev. Herbert T., J.C.D., Error Invalidating Matrimonial Consent, VII-79 pp., 1932.
83. Barrett, Rev. John D. M., S.S., J.C.D., Comparative Study of the Third Plenary Council and the Code, IX-221 pp., 1932.
84. Carberry, Rev. John J., Ph.D., S.T.D., J.C.L., The Juridical Form of Marriage, 1934.
85. Dolan, Rev. John L., A.B., J.C.L., The Defensor Vinculi, 1934.
86. Hannan, Rev. Jerome D., A.M., S.T.D., LL.B., J.C.L., The Canon Law of Wills, 1934.
87. Lemieux, Rev. Delisle A., A.M., J.C.L., The Sentence in Ecclesiastical Procedure, 1934.
88. O'Rourke, Rev. James J., A.B., J.C.L., Parish Registers, 1934.

89. TIMLIN, REV. BARTHOLOMEW, O.F.M., A.M., J.C.L., Conditional Matrimonial Consent, 1934.
90. WAHL, REV. FRANCIS X., A.B., J.C.L., The Matrimonial Impediments of Consanguinity and Affinity, 1934.
91. WHITE, REV. ROBERT J., A.B., LL.B., S.T.B., J.C.L., Canonical Ante-Nuptial Promises and the Civil Law, 1934.

www.ingramcontent.com/pod-product-compliance
Lightning Source LLC
LaVergne TN
LVHW050211080826
844660LV00012B/397
* 9 7 8 0 8 1 3 2 2 2 7 6 9 *